On Your Bike
Leicestershire & Rutland

Other areas covered in the **On Your Bike** *series include:*

BRISTOL & BATH

CHESHIRE

CHILTERNS

COTSWOLDS

DERBYSHIRE & NOTTINGHAMSHIRE

ESSEX

HERTFORDSHIRE & BEDFORDSHIRE

LANCASHIRE

LINCOLNSHIRE

NORFOLK & SURREY

SOMERSET

SURREY

THAMESSIDE

On Your Bike
Leicestershire & Rutland

Sue and Paul Thomas

COUNTRYSIDE BOOKS
NEWBURY, BERKSHIRE

First published 2003
© Sue and Paul Thomas 2003

COUNTRYSIDE BOOKS
3 Catherine Road
Newbury, Berkshire

To view our complete range of books,
please visit us at
www.countrysidebooks.co.uk

ISBN 1 85306 777 6

Designed by Graham Whiteman
Maps and photographs by the authors
Cover photo supplied by Cyclographic Publications

Typeset by Textype, Cambridge
Produced through MRM Associates Ltd., Reading
Printed in Italy

CONTENTS

AREA MAP SHOWING THE LOCATIONS OF THE RIDES

INTRODUCTION

Leicestershire and Rutland are a bit of an 'odd couple' as neighbours, Leicestershire being heavily developed and industrialised, whilst Rutland is still largely rural with an agricultural economy. Although historically distinct counties, the two were briefly combined resulting in a series of campaigns for 'independence', and a battle of the boundary signs, where locals repeatedly replaced the Leicestershire signs with Rutland ones! Today, peace and separation have returned and the Rutland County signs are legally back in place, but Leicestershire and Rutland remain closely linked.

Like the two counties, the routes in this guide offer great variety, and often marked contrasts. Quiet lanes abound, accompanied by some excellent traffic-free tracks around reservoirs, alongside canals and along disused railways, often associated with the SUSTRANS National Cycle Network. These dedicated cycling facilities are ideal locations for novice and experienced cyclists alike, but can be busy in the summer months. So, to maintain a good balance of 'hustle and bustle' and solitude, the rides described in this guide seek out the best sections of the popular cycleways and combine them with less well frequented routes. To accompany the good cycling terrain there is a rich and varied landscape with many fascinating sights and sounds along the way. Be your penchant for things historical, geographical or purely recreational you will find plenty to keep your interest as you ride along.

Those grandest of historic domestic buildings, stately homes, are on offer, including Belvoir Castle, Burley on the Hill, Cottesbrooke Hall, Melbourne Hall and the grandest of them all, Burghley House. There is also the opportunity to visit no less than three major battlefields, Empingham, Naseby and, most famously, Bosworth.

The industrial past of the area contributes much of interest, especially in Leicestershire, with windmills, canals, railways, disused furnaces and lime kilns, coal mines, ironstone mines and much more.

And for those more interested in things of a gastronomic nature there are some great places on route to eat, drink and picnic as you please, in the two counties that are home to many of England's finest foods.

Sue and Paul Thomas

GUIDE TO USING THIS BOOK

This guide consists of 20 routes of varying length, aimed at the family and leisure cyclist, rather than the hardened enthusiast, and includes areas ideal for the complete novice. However, many of the routes are close enough together to allow them to be linked to provide longer runs for the more ambitious and give a good introduction to experienced cyclists new to the area.

The route descriptions with respect to difficulty are to some extent subjective and depend upon how you approach the ride. For example, a 5-mile, off-road route is easy if taken slowly – walking up hills and avoiding obstacles – but ride at cross-country competition pace and it will be hard.

All routes start at a point where parking is available, and where possible near a rail station. Where a station is not close to the described starting point, one is usually nearby at some point on the route, and this is highlighted in the description. Rail operators normally allow bikes to be carried free of charge, though sometimes pre-booking is required and the carriage of tandems, trikes and other larger cycles may be restricted. Regulations do vary, so call and check with the relevant railway company before setting out.

Sketch maps are included, together with full route descriptions. While it should be possible to follow the routes using just this guide, it is recommended that you also carry a more detailed map. This will add to your enjoyment, and help should you stray from the route.

The sketch maps are not to scale, and the scale varies, with complicated areas requiring more detail at a larger scale. Also, to aid usability, not all detail is shown, only that which helps in following the route. Specifically, types of road junction, eg roundabout, mini roundabout, traffic light etc are not differentiated, being simply shown as a junction; the accompanying text will add further detail. In built-up areas minor junctions are not shown.

Distances are 'map-measured' and the actual distance you travel will be slightly more where hills and diversions are taken.

The route descriptions have been made as brief as possible, while still being readable. The intention is that you should be able to read and hold a fragment of description in your mind between landmarks.

Following the description are details of the major 'sights and sounds' you will encounter on your ride. There is so much to do and see in this area that not everything can be included here, and other notable attractions are mentioned in the route introductions, others are left for you to discover.

Remember, things can change, pubs close, off-road tracks deteriorate – others are repaired. So be prepared: while every care has been taken to ensure accuracy, things may not be quite as advertised!

WHEN TO GO

Leicestershire and Rutland have something to offer in all seasons, and everyone will have their own favourites. Ours are spring and autumn, with their more dramatic light and variety of foliage, plus the added bonus of smaller crowds at popular locations such as Rutland Water.

The routes in this guide generally avoid off-road tracks that are poor during winter, and so are suitable all year round. If you are planning to explore other bridleways, remember that they can be very muddy in winter and become overgrown in summer, often being at their best in the autumn and early spring.

Remember that cycling off-road on footpaths is not allowed. If you do explore stick to bridleways, byways and RUPPs (Roads Used as Public Paths), or other routes where cycling is clearly indicated as being allowed.

In terms of the best time of day, and day of the week, this varies dependent on the route. Weekends are a popular time in Rutland, which means more traffic on country roads, especially on

summer Sundays and close to tourist attractions. As anywhere, Saturdays are shopping days, and the roads around towns are busy from late morning to late afternoon.

Outside of the rush hours (especially the 'school run') the roads away from the 'A' roads and main towns are much quieter during the week, but, especially during winter, attractions may be closed or have restricted opening.

EQUIPMENT AND SAFETY

MAPS

Ordnance Survey 1:50 000 Landranger maps are best for cycling, and these are the ones generally recommended on the routes, though in a few cases the 1:25 000 Explorer sheet is used.

TRAFFIC

Being close to large centres of population you will come across traffic even on quiet lanes, and occasionally the routes in this guide by necessity follow or cross busier roads – though these are avoided wherever possible.

It is important that you know how to cycle in traffic; remember, ride confidently, and if necessary walk your bike on the pavement. Any potentially busy roads and crossings are highlighted in the text; take extra care at these points.

YOUR BIKE AND WHAT TO CARRY

The routes in this book are mostly

on road, though there are some off-road sections, and some of the less used lanes can be potholed and gravel strewn. The type of bike to use is personal preference, but in our opinion, for general leisure use the mountain bike or its less chunky cousin the hybrid offer best value for money and optimum comfort.

Make sure your bike is well maintained and safe; it is easier than trying to fix a broken bike miles from anywhere. There are, however, repairs you need to be prepared for, the main one being a puncture. The chance of a puncture can be reduced by ensuring that tyres are not under inflated, but, especially off-road, you will eventually succumb. So, carry a spare tube, tyre levers, and a small pump, it is also worth carrying instant repair patches in case you should have more than one puncture to deal with.

After punctures, the most common problems relate to things coming loose, the chain breaking, frayed cables snapping, or spokes breaking. Good maintenance will prevent all. These things are not frequent occurrences, so don't be put off, but for peace of mind you may want to look at the various multi-tools on the market. These are very compact and light, and can handle most emergency jobs.

A bicycle maintenance book, (Haynes do a very good one) will explain how to effect repairs and show you how to do at least the more simple maintenance jobs on

your bike and will quickly pay for itself.

There are various bag and pannier systems available to carry your tools and spares, together with food, camera, spare clothing etc. This is easier and less restrictive than using a rucksack, though this is very much a matter of personal preference. Bottle cages will carry your water bottles. Remember to take enough water and refill as required – on a hot summer's day dehydration can become apparent surprisingly quickly.

CLOTHING

Clothing needs to be non-restrictive and comfortable, and there should be nothing loose to become entangled with moving parts. There are two pieces of specialist cycling gear you may want to consider from the outset. Firstly, padded cycling shorts: they can make a great difference to comfort on a day in the saddle. Secondly, waterproofs: good, breathable, waterproofs are a must unless you are sure of fine weather (in England?). Cycling-specific versions are cut to cover the lower back without getting in the way when dismounting, but any good breathable-fabric jacket will suffice.

A cycling helmet is recommended. There is much debate around this subject and helmet use is not compulsory, but there is evidence that helmets do reduce the severity of injuries sustained and save lives. We always wear ours.

History along the Lincolnshire border

20 miles

The border of Rutland and Lincolnshire is rich in history from Roman through to modern times. This route visits many such examples where it is interesting to stop and speculate about the lives of those that passed by many years ago – from the Roman centurions guarding the route north at Great Casterton, the Norman stonemasons working on Tickencote church, and those who fought and died at the battle of Empingham in the War of the Roses, through to those still living today who saw *The Mallard* set its 126mph record in 1938. One wonders what they'd make of the area and its inhabitants today. The quiet lanes and peaceful villages *en route* give plenty of time for reflection.

Maps: OS Landranger 130 and 141

Starting point: Pickworth, roadside parking near the church. GR 989138

By train: There is no station on the route; the nearest is Stamford on the Peterborough to Leicester line, from where the route can be joined at Great Casterton by following the B1081 for 2½ miles.

Refreshments: There are few facilities *en route*, but recommended pub stops are the Hare and Hounds in Greatford, the Blue Bell in Belmesthorpe or the Green Dragon in Ryhall. The Blue Bell at Belmesthorpe is an old and largely unspoiled village pub with good food and local beer. It has a small garden for the summer and an open fire in the winter. Food is generally served from 12 noon till 2 pm and 6.30 pm to 9.30 pm except Sunday evenings. The bar is open all day on Sundays and bank holidays and children are welcome. The Green Dragon at Ryhall is also a very interesting building, incorporating a 13th-century cellar, said to have belonged to the original manor house.

The route: This is 20 miles with some hills, but the going is generally easy. Although the route largely avoids traffic, there are a couple of busy road sections near Ryhall and Great Casterton.

Locate the old limekiln on the edge of the village beyond the church in a small grassy recess and from there head into the village, passing the church, arch and information board on the left. **Turn L** at the junction opposite a byway, and in ¼ mile **turn R** by the Grange, signed for Ryhall and Essendine.

Turn R at the next junction and after approximately 1½ miles go

The river Gwash at Belmesthorpe

straight across at a junction with the busy B1176 and after about 2 miles arrive at the A6121 in Carlby. **Turn R** and just past Eastern Farm Implements on the right, **turn L**, heading for Greatford, which is reached in 2½ miles.

Turn R and leave Greatford, passing the Hare and Hounds on the left. Continue for 1½ miles to cross the main East Coast rail line at a level crossing and after a further ¾ mile at a junction **turn R** and then immediately **L** signed for Belmesthorpe. In Belmesthorpe **turn R** onto Shepherds Walk, signed for Ryhall, passing the Blue Bell on the left.

Continue into Ryhall and **turn L** to cross the bridge over the river Gwash and **turn R** in front of the Green Dragon.

Turn R at the junction with the A6121 **with care**, go though the traffic lights then **first L, and L again** heading for Great Casterton.

Pass a minor left turn to Tolethorpe Hall and Little Casterton, the hall being occasionally glimpsed in the trees away to the left. Also note the roadside nature reserve, so don't picnic or park your bikes here. Arrive in Great Casterton with the earthwork remains of the Roman settlement in view on the left.

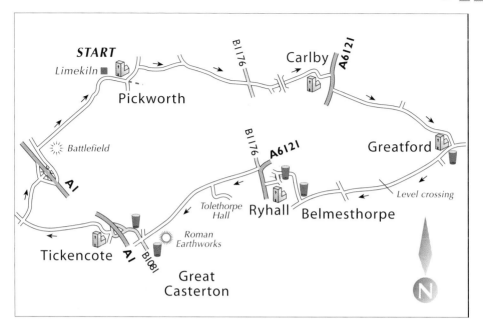

At the junction **turn R** onto the B1081, signed for the A1 and Grantham. Follow the B road under the A1 and continue as if to join the A1 North, but **turn L** for Tickencote just before the A road. Turn **immediately** L to visit the historic church in this pretty village before continuing on towards Empingham.

At a crossroads **turn R** and shortly keep with the minor road passing under the A1 then **turn L**, signed for Pickworth. Run parallel with the A1, turning **first R** at a minor junction towards Pickworth.

This is the area where the battle of Empingham took place – note the information board on the left a little way up the lane.

The lane continues, passing through a small area of parkland, where **take care** on the rough cattle grids, and on into Pickworth village, passing the limekiln on the left.

● ●

PICKWORTH
This is the site of the Battle of Loosecoat Field. The Lancastrians were defeated, and the Lincolnshire and Rutland men fighting on the losing side under the Pickworth squire Sir John Hussey fled through the village. On doing so they tore off their coats, which bore his colours, so providing the name of the battle.

PICKWORTH LIME KILN
The 'peasant poet', John Clare worked as a lime-burner in Pickworth in the early 1800s and wrote a poem about the ruins of Pickworth.

Tickencote churchyard

THE MALLARD

The main London–Edinburgh line runs through Essendine, and it was just north of the village on Stoke Bank that the famous steam locomotive *The Mallard* made the record of 126mph on 3rd July 1938. The railway hotel is still in existence as a pub.

BELMESTHORPE

The name of this village derives from the farm (Thorpe) of the Le Bolour family (12th century). The Pierreponts of Ryhall Hall owned the entire village until Mr West purchased it in 1950. The estate was then split up and most of the houses and farms were sold to the tenants. Legend has it that 'Belmisthorpe' (as it was spelt until the mid 1950s) was once larger than Ryhall and that Lady Godiva stayed at the Blue Bell Inn. The village still has two dovecotes, one

of which once acted as food store for the squire.

RYHALL

The church has associations with the 7th-century cult of St Tibba, who is supposed to have had a cell there.

GREAT CASTERTON

This village is also known as Bridge Casterton and takes its name from a Roman fort to the north of the village, and the 'bridge' carrying the Great North Road over the river Gwash to the west of the Roman road. The A1 now provides a bypass for the village.

TICKENCOTE CHURCH

Tickencote is probably the best known of all the churches in Rutland due to its elaborately carved Norman arch, which is so heavy it has sagged in the middle.

Stamford and Burghley House, where four counties meet

6½ miles

Stamford has been described as an almost perfect Georgian town, and while it has been developed considerably around its outskirts, its heart remains largely unchanged. Churches and coaching inns abound, testifying to the rich past of the town, being a popular overnight stop for coaches on the Great North Road and an important centre for trade. This ride first follows the river Welland through meadows and away from the bridge that accounts for Stamford's location, then climbs out of the valley with views over the town, before returning via the grand stately home of Burghley.

Map: OS Landranger 141

Starting point: Stamford railway station on the Peterborough to Leicester line (GR 028066). Parking at the railway station is for rail users only but alternative parking is available nearby adjacent to the meadow.

Refreshments: Stamford is a busy town with plenty of cafés, pubs, restaurants and shops. The Blue Bell at Easton on the Hill is passed approximately half-way round the route and has a pleasant garden.

The route: A short, almost entirely off-road route where the counties of Rutland, Lincolnshire, Northamptonshire and Cambridgeshire meet. A couple of busy roads are encountered but there is a footpath alternative for small children, making this an ideal, easy family outing with interest maintained throughout. The off-road sections are rough in parts and may be muddy after wet weather, but should present few problems during the summer. There is one steep climb up to Easton on the Hill.

From the station follow Graseley Drive to a car park by toilets where **turn L** to cross the footbridge onto the meadow. Dismount, as this is not a bridleway, and follow the path to a second footbridge. Do not cross this footbridge but **turn L** by the information board and go diagonally across the field, now on a bridleway, aiming for a small bridle gate in the fence opposite.

Continue on the bridle route across the meadow, following a more or less straight line rather than sticking to the bank of the river, passing *en route* the Roman ford where the road from London to

Stamford from across the meadows

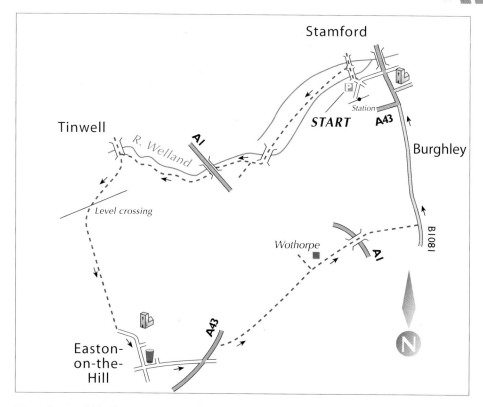

Lincoln and York once crossed the river Welland.

Cross the metal Broadeng bridge and continue on the bridleway to the right, now on the opposite bank of the river.

Keep right, and with the river, where the Hereward Way bears off to the left and shortly after, note the Stamford Spa and Mineral Iron Water Spring on the right. Continue by the weir and pumping station before passing under the busy A1, still on the riverbank. Note that this river for much of its length is the boundary between Rutland and Cambridgeshire, and the Rutland boundary sign can be seen above on the A1, with Stamford behind being in Lincolnshire.

Beyond the A1 the bridleway continues along the riverbank, with the huge Ketton cementworks coming into view. The riverbank provides a remarkable contrast to the noisy A1 behind and the industrial scene ahead. Note also the view to the left and behind to the four towers of Wothorpe House, which is visited later on the route. Take care on the last bend of the bridleway before reaching

17

The spendid ruins of Wothorpe House

Tinwell as the path here is quite narrow and close to the river.

At a junction with a bridleway by a bridge, **turn L** on the bridleway that shortly swings to the right onto an enclosed green lane by a small Northamptonshire boundary sign. Here the route designation changes to byway, a symptom of the varying approaches to clarifying rights of way between different county councils.

Cross the railway line with care at Tinwell Crossing and start the climb up to Easton on the Hill. The climb is on a loose but good track surface and the worst is soon over. The views to Stamford away to the left and below add interest during the climb.

On entering the village pass on the left first the imposing Glebe House, where Captain Lancelot Skynner of HMS *Lutine*, source of the Lutine Bell, lived in around 1775, and then the National Trust-owned Priests' House.

Turn L at a small crossroads onto High Street and pass the Blue Bell on the left. After passing through the village, the wooded Spring Close on the right is ideal for a picnic.

At the junction with the main road **turn L**, noting the path on the left, and in approximately 100 yards **turn R** with care onto the bridleway for Wothorpe.

The bridleway is initially quite

narrow and overgrown in summer but the surface is good throughout, and on reaching woodland the track becomes wider and altogether more pleasant.

At a bridleway junction by the ruins of Wothorpe House continue straight on, following the broad track with further views of the ruins to the left and Stamford below.

Cross the bridge over the A1 and continue to the old Great North Road where you **turn L** towards St Martins Without – which is the part of Stamford lying in Cambridgeshire. Note the footpath on the right hand side of the road if needed for small children and descend the hill. Pass one of the main gates to Burghley House, giving pedestrian access to the deer park, and continue passing some of Stamford's finest buildings, and restaurants. Pass below the gallows spanning the street and carrying the George Hotel sign and **turn L** at the traffic lights, signed for long-stay parking, to return to the station and car park.

● ●

STAMFORD SPA
Stamford Spa was brought into use in 1819 and was apparently much sought after by persons afflicted by various ailments in the belief that the water had medicinal properties. The stone head was placed by order of John Paradise in 1864. The spa was renovated in 1994.

PRIESTS' HOUSE
A key can be obtained from local addresses to view the Priests' House, a pre-Reformation building of special architectural interest housing a small museum of village bygones.

WOTHORPE HOUSE
Wothorpe House was one of the best lodges of its time when built in 1610 by Thomas Cecil (1542–1622), the 1st Earl of Exeter as a retreat for himself when Burghley was being spring-cleaned. It was built on the plan of a Greek cross and has four corner towers. It now lies in splendid ruins.

BURGHLEY HOUSE AND PARK
Burghley is probably best known for the horse trials held here annually. It is the largest and grandest house of the first Elizabethan age, built by William Cecil between 1565 and 1587 and still occupied by his descendants. As well as the impressive house, there is a 160 acre deer park and orangery restaurant, both designed by Capability Brown, plus a sculpture garden and 18th-century music collection. The house is generally open from Easter until the end of October, and the park is open all year for walking and picnicking.

STAMFORD
Situated in South Kesteven, Lincolnshire, Stamford was proclaimed as 'the finest stone town in England' and declared a conservation area in 1967. It occupies a strategic point being around halfway between London and York on the Great North Road. By the 14th century, Stamford was one of the richest towns in England, its wealth based on the wool industry and exports of pottery and finished cloth. It reached new heights of prosperity when stagecoaches ruled the roads and the town supplied much needed refreshments and accommodation in its hostelries, many of which are still standing.

From Rutland Water North

20 miles plus 7½ miles for the peninsula loop

The creation of Rutland Water by the flooding of the Gwash Valley has made not just a spectacular beauty spot and birdlife sanctuary, but also a top class cycling facility. This ride (and route 4) takes in some of the best sections of the justifiably popular round-the-reservoir cycle route, but also give some respite from the crowds, including a visit to Oakham, the county town of Rutland, and the unspoilt estate village of Exton. The optional loop around the Hambleton Peninsula on returning to the reservoir offers arguably the best off-road cycling in the area, so remember to save some energy!

Maps: OS Landranger 141 and 130

Starting point: The Rutland Water pay and display car park at Whitwell. GR 924082

By train: From Oakham station the route can easily be joined on the outskirts of Oakham.

Refreshments: There are pubs in several of the villages *en route*, including Exton and Cottesmore, and Oakham has all the facilities you'd expect of Rutland's county town. Cafés can also be found at the Rutland Railway Museum and at the car park in Whitwell. Also in Whitwell is the Noel Arms an ideal place to relax on completion of the ride.

The route: A mixture of road and off-road with some short hills makes this a moderately hard route, even harder if the highly recommended Hambleton Peninsula loop is included. The cycleway around Rutland Water is very popular with both cyclists and walkers, and on summer weekends progress can be very slow. The Hambleton Peninsula is less heavily used, but the final section of this route, from the A606 to Whitwell, can be very busy, so take care and remember to give way to pedestrians. The track surface off road is generally good, but can be loose in places and occasionally muddy.

Leave the car park by the road, signed 'vehicle exit', heading back towards Whitwell. On a sharp left-hand bend **turn R** onto the cyclepath, signed as the National Byway, and shortly afterwards cross the busy A606 **with care** to continue on a minor road. Climb and then descend past a crossroads to a 'Give Way', where you **fork R** on the National Byway into Exton.

The Hambleton peninsula

By the Fox and Hounds **turn R then L** around the green. Note the Rutland Heritage Trail information board by the pub.

As the road bends right at a 'Give Way', go straight on, joining a bridleway marked as a 'No Through Road'.

Continue to a four-way bridleway and footpath junction, where go straight ahead on a grassy bridleway. Climb and then descend to a road, where **turn R** and descend to a point between two lakes with a view to Fort Henry on the upper lakeshore.

Retrace your route from the lakes but keep with the road where the grassy bridleway followed earlier joins from the left and continue straight on at the next junction. Keep with the bridleway road where it bends sharp left, following the Viking Way briefly before **forking R** at a junction and shortly **R again** at the next junction. Meet the public road at a gate, where **turn R** and follow the road to Cottesmore.

In Cottesmore **turn L**, signed for the National Byway and Oakham. Continue passing the church, shops and pubs. After passing through the village **turn R** and **immediately L** heading towards Ashwell, on Ashwell Road, signed for the Rutland Railway Museum.

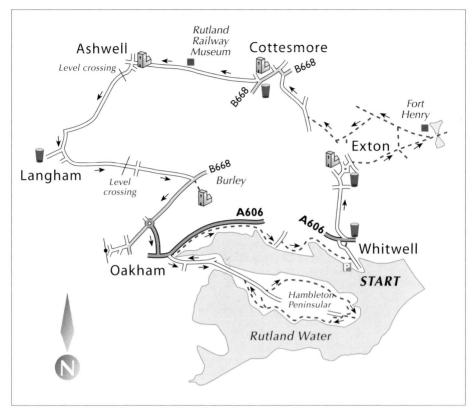

Pass the railway museum with hilltop views and descend into Ashwell, where **turn L** at the crossroads and shortly afterwards, on a sharp left bend, **turn R** with care onto Langham Road. At the level crossing, pressing the plunger will open the barrier if it's safe to cross; alternatively use the pedestrian gate **with care**.

In Langham **turn L** heading for Burley, re-cross the railway, and at the crossroads go straight on, to Langham Lane. Climb to Burley on the Hill and at a junction with the B668, cross with care to a minor road that leads to footpath access for Holy Cross church in the grounds of Burley on the Hill. The house is not open to the public. After visiting the church return to the B668, **turn L** and descend towards Oakham and a roundabout junction.

Straight on here leads into Oakham for those using the train or wishing to visit Oakham's tourist attractions. After the roundabout the station is reached via a right turn on a left bend by the earthworks close to the historic hall and church. Adjacent to the station

Fort Henry seen across the lake

is the Grainstore Brewery and Visitors Centre.

At the roundabout **turn L** onto the A6003, signed for Kettering and Uppingham; the footpath on the right is a shared-use cycleway. Continue to a T-junction where **turn L** onto the busy A606; again there is a shared-use cycle path on the right of the road. Continue a short way to a junction with the Round Rutland Water cycleway.

Turn R for the highly recommended Hambleton peninsula loop.

Ignore the right turn for Eggleton and continue on the 'No Through Road' signed for 'Hambleton Village Only' and the peninsula circular route. As the road starts to climb join the shared-use footpath on the left, joining the off-road cycleway to the left towards the top of the hill.

The cycle track around the peninsula is easily followed and signed throughout. The route is mostly good throughout, but there are some steep sections, sharp bends and occasional poor surface so take care. Note also that there is some limited vehicular access so cars may be encountered, but rarely.

On completion of the off-road loop **turn L** on rejoining the road, continuing towards the A606 junction previously visited. Just before the junction **turn R** onto the shared-use footpath, signed as the National Byway and heading for Whitwell.

Follow the tarmac shared-use path alongside the A606 until the road starts to climb, where you follow the cycleway through a gate and onto the lakeside track. Follow the signed cycle route back along the shore to Whitwell and the car park.

• •

WHITWELL PARKING AND FACILITIES

Whitwell cycle hire is open all year, with a good bike shop selling cycling accessories and bikes in addition to hiring them. Also there is a well-stocked outdoor gear shop and outdoor climbing wall. Café, toilets and tourist information are also available, but with restricted opening hours.

EXTON PARK

Exton Park has been known to have ironstone under it since the late 1800s, but it was not until 1948 that a lease to quarry was granted. Mining ceased in 1974 and the only visible signs that remain are a few steep inclines in the fields.

FORT HENRY

Fort Henry was actually built as a summerhouse to replace the old boathouse at the pond and its correct name is the Pond House. The Earl of Gainsborough used the venue for special events for his estate workers and tenants.

RUTLAND RAILWAY MUSEUM

Four miles from Oakham, in Cottesmore, is an open-air museum housing a large collection of, amongst other items, steam and diesel locomotives. It is run by volunteers and is open as a museum only most weekends and occasional weekdays. Telephone 01572 813203 at weekends to find out when trains are running. The museum tells the story of railways in industry – especially local ironstone quarrying. There is a visitor centre with light refreshments, shop and souvenirs available.

BURLEY ON THE HILL

The village of Burley on the Hill is most famous for its grand house, which is not open to the public, and there is no right of way through the grounds. The church however, is open from 10 am to 6 pm on Sundays in summer and 10 am to 5 pm in the winter. During the week the key can be borrowed from the gardener. It is maintained by the Churches Conservation Trust and is no longer used for services, but remains a consecrated building.

OAKHAM HISTORIC HALL AND CHURCH

This Norman Great Hall is part of a late 12th-century, fortified manor house, with the remains of an earlier motte and bailey castle visible. The walls are covered with unique presentation horseshoes, which were forfeited by royalty and peers of the realm to the Lord of the Manor of Oakham. The castle is now often used as a venue for marriages. It is open to the public most days.

THE VIKING WAY

The Viking Way is a long distance walk running 90 miles, from the Humber Bridge to Oakham.

4

From Rutland Water South

21 miles

Starting from the scenic south shore of Rutland Water this ride takes in one of the best sections of the round-the-reservoir cycleway before escaping the crowds across the Chater and Welland valleys. A turf maze, a medieval penance, a Victorian engineering masterpiece and the home of one of Rutland's most famous building materials are among the attractions *en route*. The return offers the chance to visit the improbably located Normanton church, jutting out into the reservoir and now housing a museum dedicated to the history of the area.

Map: OS Landranger 141

Starting point: Normanton, the pay-and-display car park. GR 930057

By train: From Oakham station the Round Rutland Water cycleway can be joined as for route 3, but then heading south via Egleton to pick up this route beyond Manton, at the junction with the road for Lyndon.

Refreshments: There is a café and shop in the car park at Normanton, and also close by is the lakeside Normanton Park Hotel, with a pleasant outdoor seating area, serving afternoon tea and bar snacks. Along the route there are pleasant pubs in several villages including the Cuckoo and the Kings Arms Hotel in Wing, both serving food and having gardens, the George and Dragon in Seaton, and the Railway Inn at Ketton.

The route: Apart from the off-road section along the reservoir shore this route sticks mainly to quiet lanes but with a couple of busy road crossings. The numerous valleys traversed make this a hilly and relatively strenuous ride.

Follow the Round Rutland Water cycleway to the west, heading away from Normanton. In approximately 2 miles keep with the cycleway as it climbs away from the shore to a road. At the junction continue straight ahead, signed for Lyndon.

In Lyndon keep straight on at the crossroads, heading for Wing;

descend into the valley bottom and **keep R** at a junction. Climb now crossing a railway bridge and at a 'Give Way' **turn R** into Wing. Immediately on entering the village **turn L** to visit the turf maze. Return from the maze and **turn L** to continue through the village passing the church, pubs and shop.

The cycleway alongside Rutland Water

Keep with the main road on leaving the village and at a sharp right bend while descending **turn L**, heading for Glaston and Bisbrooke. Cross the railway by the fishing lakes and at a fork **keep R**. Go straight on at a crossroads, cross a further small stream and climb quite steeply to the A47.

Cross the A47 with care and continue straight ahead on the minor lane into Bisbrooke. Ignore the right turn onto Top Lane and at the 'Give Way' **turn R**, signed for Lydington and Seaton. Climb briefly before descending, ignoring minor turns and passing a pub on the right. Cross the valley bottom and climb again to a crossroads to **turn L**, heading for Seaton.

Follow the ridge-top road with good views before descending slightly into Seaton, keeping with the main road, passing the church and George and Dragon freehouse. At the crossroads go straight on, heading for Barrowden, noting the views to the Seaton Viaduct below and across the Welland Valley.

Descend through a series of bends to a 'Give Way' at the B672, where you **turn L**. Climb and, where the B road goes sharp left, **turn R with care**, signed for Barrowden. The road runs level at first, before descending gradually into Barrowden.

At the 'Give Way' go straight across onto Back Road and at the next

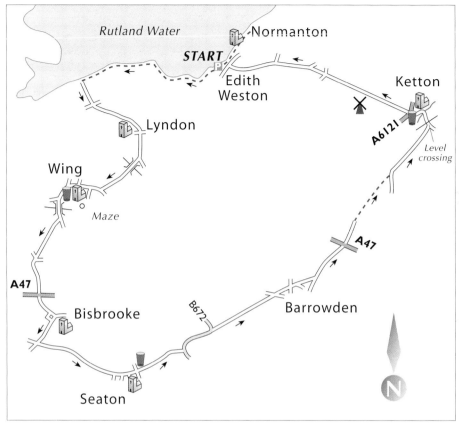

'Give Way' straight on again, heading for Wakerly and Peterborough. **Turn L** at the next junction, still heading for Peterborough, to contour the valley side and **turn L** again at the 'Give Way'. The road dips then climbs back to the A47, to **turn R and immediately L** onto a small lane marked 'Unsuitable for Motor Vehicles'. The potholed lane eventually becomes a rough track along the broad ridge top before meeting a tarmac road, where you continue straight ahead keeping to the high ground between the valleys of the Chater and the Welland.

Descend gradually into Ketton and at a 'Give Way' **turn L** and continue over the level crossing. Cross the valley of the Chater and pass the impressive Ketton church and nearby Railway Inn to a 'Give Way' at the A6121. Go straight across, signed for Empingham, and climb out of Ketton, passing a disused windmill on the left.

At a crossroads continue straight ahead for Edith Weston and at a

27

'Give Way' with the main Rutland Water South road **turn L** and very shortly **R** with care, back into the car park. Follow the cycleway to the right for a recommended detour to the museum in the very picturesque Normanton church set in the reservoir.

• •

WING TURF MAZE
Wing turf maze is circular, 40 feet in diameter and thought to be associated with religious penance. It is one of only eight of its kind in existence in England. Its design matches that of mazes depicted on ancient coins and seen on the floors of medieval French cathedrals. Medieval monks may have crawled along the winding lines; stopping at points to pray and repent. It is known that in the 12th century there was a monastery at Wing.

SEATON VIADUCT
Also known as the Harringworth Viaduct, this 82-arch, ¼ mile-long, brick-built railway viaduct was constructed between 1876 and 1878 to carry the LMS Kettering to Manton branch line. Over 2,000 men worked on the viaduct using approximately 20 million bricks. The St Pancras to Nottingham service used to stop at Manton station to pick up members of the hunting fraternity.

KETTON AND COLLYWESTON
Ketton and Collyweston are the sources of the two main Rutland traditional building materials, Ketton stone for building and Collyweston slate for roofing.

EDITH WESTON
Edith was the wife of Edward the Confessor from 1045. She was also the daughter of Godwin of Wessex and Harold II's sister. Due to a feud between Edward and Godwin, Edith was deprived of her lands and banished to a monastery in Hampshire. She subsequently died in 1072, but not before being restored to favour in 1052. On her death ownership of the lands passed to the king of England, who prefixed the name Weston with Edith in her memory.

NORMANTON CHURCH MUSEUM
This museum started life as the church of St Matthew when it was completed in 1826. Then in 1975 the floor was raised by 3 metres, and an embankment built to save it from flooding at the time the reservoir was filled with water. Nowadays it houses a history of the reservoir ranging from dinosaur fossils and Anglo-Saxon skeletons to press cuttings and videos of the reservoir construction. The museum is open every day from Easter to September, and weekends in the winter; there is a gift shop.

5

The Rutland Watershed

21 miles

A route around the upper reaches of the river Chater and the highest ground in Rutland. Several rivers rise in these hills, including the Chater and Eyebrook draining to the east, and the Sence and Queniborough Brook draining to the west. So should you be unfortunate enough to encounter rain, cheer yourself up by working out which of it will end up in the North Sea via the Wash, and which in the Irish Sea via the Bristol Channel. This is a ride with a surprisingly wild feel to it, with few popular attractions and facilities *en route*, but with splendid views and ample opportunities for solitude.

Map: OS Landranger 141

Starting point: Tilton on the Hill; on-road parking on the old Melton road off the junction near the church. GR 743057

By train: From Oakham the route can be joined at Braunston-in-Rutland.

Refreshments: There are few facilities on the route, but there is a shop and pub at the start in Tilton on the Hill, and a pub in Braunston-in-Rutland.

The route: Several climbs and a rough off-road section make this a moderately hard outing. Much of the off-road is on good track, but the initial section is across open fields and may be muddy in places during winter.

From the parking return to the junction and follow Main Street, with the church on the left, heading towards Loddington, and at a junction **keep L** with Loddington Road. **Keep R** at the junction in front of Robin-a-Tiptoe Hill, cross a bridge over a disused railway and then keep straight on at the crossroads by Oxey Farm where the National Cycle Network routes 63 and 64 cross.

Keep with the road to the left through Loddington, heading for Launde, and continue straight on at the next junction still heading for Launde. A short climb then leads to a descent beyond a cattle grid into Launde Park, passing Launde Abbey on the right.

At the next junction continue straight ahead and over the cattle grid, heading for Withcote and Braunston. Shortly **turn R** onto a bridleway signed for Belton on the Leicestershire Round. Go through

The Upper Chater Valley

the gate, following the blue waymark on a yellow post and climb the rough track above the lake to the left to another waymarked gate. Continue in the direction of the waymark across the open field to the gate on the opposite side, contouring slightly to the right to avoid dropping into the small intervening valley.

At the next gate again cross open fields, initially following the well-marked sheep track and then maintaining the same course keeping just above the left-hand wooded field edge to reach an obvious way-marked gate in the bottom field corner. Go through the gate and follow the narrow path over the stream and **turn R** with the fence. Cross another small stream and follow the track as it bends to the left and makes a short climb to a three-way bridleway junction. **Turn R** here along the field edge; still keeping the fence to your right.

Shortly the track levels out and then descends slightly to another footpath bridleway junction, to **turn R** onto the well-made track. Re-cross the stream and pass through a small bridlegate and then make a long gradual climb to the ridge top and a four-way bridleway junction; **turn L** here staying with the well-made track.

The track is then followed in a generally straight line keeping to the high ground and with good views over the Chater Valley. Pass barns where the track turns to

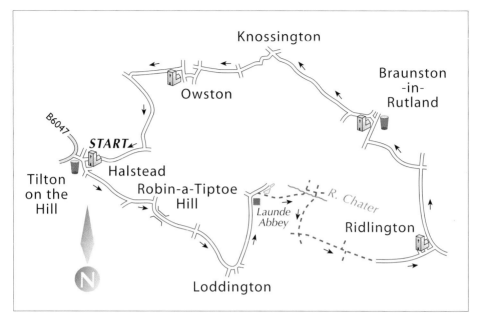

tarmac and ignore crossing bridleways to arrive at farm buildings and houses, where the bridleway becomes public highway.

Follow this road, with continuing views, to Ridlington, where keep with the main road and at a 'Give Way' **turn L**, heading for Braunston. Two valley crossings then lead to a crossroads, where **turn L**, signed for Braunston. Ignore minor no through roads to right and left to arrive in Braunston. Pass the church and **turn L**, heading for Knossington by the Blue Ball, and at the next junction **turn L** again, still heading for Knossington.

Shortly after leaving Braunston, and where the road bends sharp left, **turn R with care**, signed for

Knossington. The road weaves pleasantly to Knossington, where **turn L** and immediately **L again** on Owston Road. Go straight ahead at the next junction, keeping with the main road and still heading for Owston. At the 'Give Way' **turn L**, signed for Owston and Tilton, and just after the Owston village sign take the **first R** signed for Marefield. At the next junction **turn R**, signed for Marefield, and **keep L** with the road at the next junction still heading for Marefield.

Just after a sharp left-hand bend **fork L** signed for Halstead, and at the next junction **turn R**, heading for Tilton. Climb through Halstead passing the entrance to Halstead Farm Trail on the right, and so back to adjacent Tilton on the Hill.

Launde Abbey

ROBIN-A-TIPTOE HILL

This hill gets its name from a rather gruesome story. A sheepstealer was strung up and left to hang on the hill, but he was not hoisted high enough. He stood on tiptoe until the coast was clear and his friends were able to return and cut him down. The hill has borne his name ever since.

LAUNDE ABBEY

The abbey is actually an Elizabethan manor house now run as a Leicester diocesan retreat house and conference centre. The community of five and daily staff of twenty who look after the house welcome individuals of all religions and cultures as well as organizations from churches, charities, schools, colleges etc. The chapel is open to members of the public at certain times.

HALSTEAD HOUSE FARM

Here there is a nature trail, farm animals, pony rides, tractor and trailer rides, indoor and outdoor play areas, and pedal tractors. There is also a farm machinery museum and farm shop. It is open from April to September 10 am to 5.30 pm except Mondays and bank holidays.

Hallaton and Eyebrook Reservoir

24 miles

The peaceful area of rolling hills along the Leicestershire/Rutland border to the east of the bird sanctuary of Eyebrook Reservoir is understandably very popular with local cyclists. The light traffic and tucked away places all add to the appeal. Good cycling and interesting villages are found throughout the ride, but Medbourne, with its green, four bridges and impressive church, will be remembered and the road from Cranoe to Goadby via Glooston is a particular delight to cycle.

Map: OS Landranger 141

Starting point: The parking point below Stoke Dry by the woodland on the north-east shore of Eyebrook Reservoir. There is also a small amount of roadside car parking along the reservoir shore. GR 853964

By train: From Market Harborough, where the route can be joined at Slawston via Great Bowden and Welham (see route 12).

Refreshments: There are few facilities *en route* but there are pubs in several of the villages passed through. These include the Fox Inn at Hallaton, which has a restaurant, children's play area and beer garden serving food both lunchtimes and evenings, and the Old Barn Inn on Andrews Lane in Glooston, a 16th-century former coaching inn with an à la carte menu specialising in fresh seafood.

The route: All on minor roads with little traffic, but several long and steep climbs make this a moderately hard ride. On summer weekends the reservoir is popular and parked cars may cause congestion, necessitating care.

From the parking point follow the reservoir side and cross the Eye Brook at a bridge to a T-junction, where **turn L** to follow the southwest shore. After approximately 1½ miles the road climbs away from the reservoir to a T-junction, where **turn L** and descend into Great Easton. **Turn R** by the green in the centre of the village, heading for Drayton and Bringhurst.

At the next junction continue for Drayton, and climb gradually through the village and on to Medbourne. **Turn R** in this pretty village by the green and then **first**

Eyebrook reservoir

L by the church and through a seasonal ford, only flooded after very heavy rain. Shortly **turn L** again and after a short steep climb **turn R**, heading for Slawston.

In Slawston **turn L**, signed for Cranoe, pass through the village and after ¾ mile **turn L** at a T-junction. Continue to a crossroads, where **turn R** into Cranoe village, signed for Glooston, and climb steeply, passing the church before descending into Glooston.

In Glooston **turn R** for Goadby, signed as a gated road, to pass through pleasant undulating scenery. A steep descent and re-ascent leads to Goadby, where **turn** R to reach a T-junction and **turn R** again, heading for Hallaton.

Keep with the contouring road for approximately 2 miles to a T-junction, where **turn R** and climb to the day's high point before sweeping down into Hallaton, where **turn L and L again**, signed for Horninghold.

Just after passing through Horninghold **turn R** and climb, heading back towards Great Easton. At a junction with the B664 go straight ahead, and in about 2 miles reach the junction above Eyebrook Reservoir visited on the outward route. **Turn L** and shortly descend to reach the reservoir and so return to the car park.

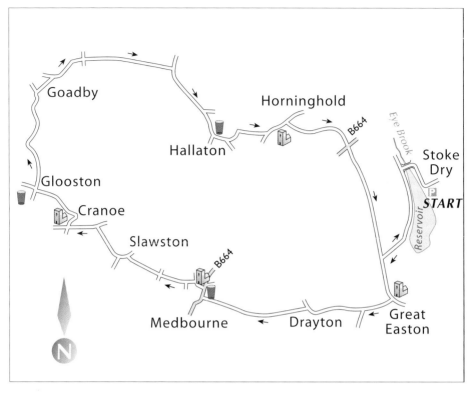

ST ANDREW'S CHURCH, STOKE DRY

St Andrew's church was largely rebuilt in the 13th century and dates from at least the Norman period. Legend has it that the priest's room, found via a narrow staircase from the north aisle of the church, provided the meeting place for the hatching of The Gunpowder Plot. Interestingly, Sir Everard Digby, one of the famous plotters, has a family tomb in the church.

EYEBROOK RESERVOIR

The reservoir was built between 1937 and 1940 to supply Corby steelworks. It is now owned by British Steel and has been run as a trout fishery since 1942. The reservoir, listed as a Site of Special Scientific Interest, is a bird sanctuary attracting many bird-watching enthusiasts. A far cry from its use by the 617 squadron (the dambusters) to practise for their raid on Mohne Dam!

HALLATON

Hallaton has had a 'hare pie scramble and bottle kicking' taking place on Easter Monday since medieval times. Nowadays, however, the pie is more likely to be made of beefsteak and the bottles are small barrels which contain beer! The contest is between the Hallatonians and their neighbours from Medbourne. There are processions led by various local bands and the whole event is meticulously planned.

Medbourne

HALLATON VILLAGE MUSEUM

This award winning museum set in one of Leicestershire's most historic villages has exhibits relating to local history including the 'bottle kicking'. Entry is free (donations welcomed) and the museum is open weekends and bank holidays from 2.30 pm till 5 pm, May to October.

RUTLAND

Rutland covers 150 square miles, is approximately 20 miles across and had a population of 37,800 in 2002. As such it is England's smallest county and so it`s motto *Multum in Parvo* (much in little) seems appropriate. In Anglo-Saxon times it was known as Rota's Land. An old English King subsequently appropriated the county and a great deal of it remained royal land until the 16th century.

The Windmills of Wymondham and Whissendine

25 miles

Two splendid windmills, both in the process of restoration and open to the public, are among the highlights on this rolling route around the headwaters of the River Eye. The windmills of Whissendine, in Rutland, and Wymondham, in Leicestershire, stand at almost identical elevations facing each other across the valley and county boundary, a valley that also has interest in terms of transport history. Here lie the remains of the Oakham Canal that extended the Wreake Navigation at Melton Mowbray by 15 miles into Rutland, and so linked Oakham to the Grand Union. Here also, and still in use, is the Leicester to Peterborough railway, the scene of controversy in the 1840s when the Earl of Harborough vigorously and violently opposed the passage of the railway over his land at Stapleford Park. The Earl, a shareholder in the previously mentioned Oakham Canal, no doubt knew the railway would spell the end for that already struggling venture.

Map: OS Landranger 130

Starting point: In the centre of Wymondham village, near The Berkley Arms – on-road parking. GR 852188

By train: From Melton Mowbray the route can be joined where it crosses the B676 near Stapleford, this entails following the busy B676 from Melton Mowbray for approximately 4 miles.

Refreshments: In Wymondham there is a café and shop at the windmill, and the Berkeley Arms by the start of the route; there are also shops and pubs in Whissendine. Pubs of note passed on the way are the Marquis of Granby and the Royal Horseshoes just off-route in Waltham on the Wolds, the Tollemache Arms in Buckminster and the cyclist-friendly Blue Dog in Sewstern.

The route: The route sticks mostly to quiet lanes, but one short stretch of the busy B676 is used. This combined with the distance and many rolling climbs make it unsuitable for novice cyclists.

From the junction by the Berkeley Arms head towards Edmonthorpe and shortly **turn R** onto Edmonthorpe Road. In just over ¾ mile **turn R**, signed 'gated road', for Whissendine Station (now closed). Descend and briefly run alongside the disused canal before arriving at a junction; **turn R** and go over the level crossing at what used to be Whissendine Station, then **turn L**, signed for Whissendine, crossing the Rutland boundary.

On entering Whissendine **turn R** opposite the Methodist chapel and Rutland Heritage Trail information board. Descend, passing the church and pubs, cross the river and climb to a junction for Stapleford. Take the **next R** signed for Melton to visit the Whissendine windmill. The entrance is on the left in between the houses.

Return to the junction for Stapleford, **turn L** and follow the road to Stapleford and Stapleford Park, keeping the park on the right. Cross the railway and **turn R** on the B676 through Saxby and, in Garthope, after passing the church and signed for Waltham, **turn L** to leave the B road.

Cross two shallow valleys and then climb, passing a large transmitter on the left. Just past the watertower and smaller transmitter on the edge of Waltham on the Wolds **turn R** for Stonesby, or continue into the village for a pub stop.

Follow the road through Stonesby village, and shortly **turn L** to Saltby, where **turn R** to Sproxton and on to Buckminster.

In Buckminster take the **immediate L** onto Back Street, just before the

junction with the B676. Follow the road, passing the church on the left to a junction, where **turn R** opposite an impressive gatehouse, and then **turn L** onto the B676 and **immediately R**. At a junction in Sewstern **turn R** for Wymondham; the Blue Dog is on the left. In approximately 2 miles, where the road bends sharp left, **turn R**, signed for Garthope, and at the next junction **turn L** and shortly L **again** to descend into Wymondham, passing the windmill on the right.

WHISSENDINE WINDMILL
The mill is presently powered by an electric motor but the intention is to return to sail power as soon as possible. It is fully working and very busy supplying flour to a number of outlets. It is open to the public if the miller is present and working, which is most of the time.

WYMONDHAM WINDMILL
This windmill is also the site of craft shops and tearooms. The mill is unusual in being one of only four six-sailed windmills remaining in the country and is in the process of being restored. The village of Wymondham is reputed to be the home of Stilton cheese.

STAPLEFORD PARK
Stapleford Park Country House Hotel, Spa, Golf and Sporting Estate is thought to be the finest and most beautiful example of an English stately home. It also boasts an historic walled garden. The church of St Mary Magdalene situated in the gardens is now used only for special events and weddings.

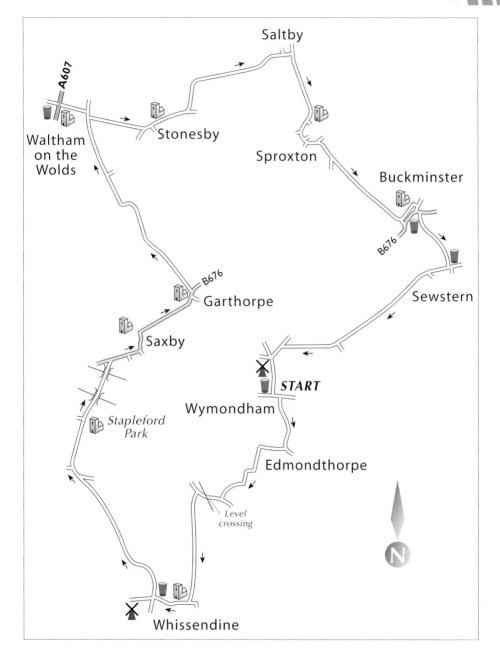

Saltby

A607

Stonesby

Waltham
on the
Wolds

Sproxton

Buckminster

B676

Sewstern

B676

Garthorpe

Saxby

START

Stapleford
Park

Wymondham

Edmondthorpe

Level
crossing

N

Whissendine

Buckminster church, hidden away on Back Street

Belvoir Castle and The Vale of Belvoir

13½ miles

Starting from the historic Rutland Arms by the Grantham Canal, the route climbs out of the Vale of Belvoir towards Belvoir Castle, which dominates the view for much of the ride. A circuit of the hills around Knipton Reservoir in the valley of the River Devon then follows before returning to the Vale and a delightful canal side section of the Sustrans National Cycle Network Route 15.

Map: OS Landranger 130

Starting point: North of Woolsthorpe By Belvoir, parking beyond the canal and railway bridge, close to the Rutland Arms public house. GR 844351

By train: From the rail station at Bottesford on the Grantham to Nottingham line, the starting point of the route can be reached in 3½ miles on minor roads heading for Woolsthorpe By Belvoir via Muston and Stenworth.

Refreshments: The Rutland Arms near the start of the route is very popular, family friendly and even has camping facilities and jet wash! Belvoir Castle has a shop, tearoom and restaurant, and there are pubs *en route* in Branston, Croxton-Kerrial and Denton.

The route: A moderately easy route on a mixture of quiet lanes and off-road track, but with a couple of long climbs. The off-road section on the National Cycle Network is generally in good condition all year, but the track between Branston and Croxton Kerrial is rough in places and may be muddy after wet weather.

Pass the Rutland Arms on the right and continue back along the road to a junction where **turn L**, with Belvoir Castle dominating the view ahead. Continue to a crossroads in Woolsthorpe By Belvoir and **turn R**, signed for Belvoir, with continuing views of the castle to the left and across the vale of Belvoir to the right.

Pass the parking and entrance to Belvoir Castle and in approximately 1 mile at a junction **turn R** towards Eastwell and Melton. Take care, as these normally quiet roads can be quite busy when Belvoir Castle is open. Continue to a crossroads and **turn L**, signed for Branston and Waltham. A long gradual descent then leads to a bridge with a

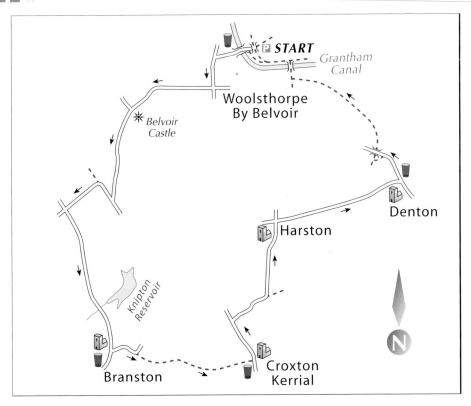

glimpse of Knipton Reservoir over to the left. Climb then into Branston, pass the church and the Wheel Inn and immediately **turn L**, signed Knipton and Belvoir Castle.

After a short climb and on a sharp left-hand bend, **turn R** onto a rough track, ignoring the green arrow marking a footpath going sharper right. The track leads past barns on the right and continues climbing gently before descending and crossing the undulating valley bottom. Pass alongside a sewage treatment plant to the left and a small wood on the right, where the track becomes a concrete road.

Ignore an overgrown right of way to the right after passing the wood and continue on the concrete track to climb into Croxton Kerrial.

The track turns to tarmac as it enters the village and leads to a road junction, where **turn L**. A right turn here leads to the pub. Pass the church on the right and after leaving the village **turn R** at a junction signed for Harston, noting the views to Belvoir Castle on the left. Cross the steep-sided valley and at a 'Give Way' in Harston **turn R** onto Main Street towards Denton.

Looking across the Vale of Belvoir

Continue into Denton, where **turn L** and shortly after, at a bridge, descend to join a spur of the Sustrans National Cycle Network Route 15, signed for the Rutland Arms and Woolsthorpe by Belvoir. Follow the signed route, eventually crossing the Grantham Canal and joining the main NCN Route 15, where **turn L**. Shortly at a Millennium milepost where Route 15 goes right for Nottingham on a disused railway, stick with the canal bank for Woolsthorpe By Belvoir to emerge by the Rutland Arms.

BELVOIR CASTLE

This grand 19th-century castle and Leicestershire home of the Duke and Duchess of Rutland, houses one of the finest collections of art works in private hands. 'Belvoir' actually means beautiful view, an extremely apt name for the position of the castle on the hill. The castle is open to the public between the hours of 11 am and 5 pm, May to September daily, and in October on Sundays only. There is also a rose garden, statue garden, artpark, adventure playground, maze, shop, tearooms and a licensed restaurant. Note – the car park is open only the ticket office is open and only for visitors to the castle. Also, the castle closes for functions so it's always worth checking on this.

HEDGEROWS

The hedgerows alongside the track into Croxton Kerrial are ancient and varied, with many blackthorns for sloe gin makers.

A lock on the Grantham Canal

GRANTHAM CANAL

The Grantham Canal travels 33 miles and crosses three counties from Grantham through the heart of the Vale of Belvoir to the River Trent near Nottingham. The Grantham Grand Canal cycle route is a 15 mile circular route starting and finishing at Hinckley canal basin, following towpaths and quiet country lanes.

9

Villages north of Melton Mowbray

22 miles

Setting out from the home of Stilton cheese and the famous Melton Mowbray pork pie, this ride takes you into the hills rising above the Vale of Belvoir. This is an area of industrial as well as culinary heritage, with several branches of dismantled railway and old ironstone workings in evidence at Holwell that fed a blast furnace in the valley below. More recently coal was extracted at the nearby Asfordby 'super-pit', which closed in 1997 after a very brief production life. Now the area is largely tranquil away from the main roads and a pleasant contrast to the busy town of Melton.

Map: OS Landranger 129

Starting point: Melton Mowbray railway station where there is pay-and-display parking that is not restricted to rail users. Plenty of alternative parking is available in Melton Mowbray, including by the cattle market which avoids much of the town traffic, but does mean missing the splendid church. GR 753187

By train: From Melton Mowbray railway station.

Refreshments: Melton Mowbray has a large selection of shops, cafés, pubs and restaurants. There are also pubs in many of the villages, including the Rose and Crown and Black Horse just off the route in Hose and the Nags Head and White Hart in Harby, where there is also a filling station selling snacks and drinks.

The route: Although the majority of this route is on quiet roads through pretty villages there are a couple of busy road sections and the traffic in Melton Mowbray requires care. Along with several minor ups and downs there are two main climbs: the long gradual climb out of Melton at the start, and the steeper climb back into the hills from the Vale of Belvoir at Stathern.

From the station follow the road to the exit, and shortly before meeting the A606 **turn L** onto a gravel track signed for toilets. This leads to a car park and recreation ground where dismount and **turn R** on the footpath marked with a 'no cycling' sign. Continue straight on behind the church through the churchyard onto a minor road and to a junction with the A606. Dismount again and cross to the pedestrian area, continuing straight ahead to follow South Parade to the left.

At the next junction **bear R**, signed for the cattle market, pass the Half

A cobbled street in Melton Mowbray

Moon pub and the Bell Shopping Centre to join a minor road by the Kings Head. Go straight ahead to the traffic lights, where continue straight across onto Scalford Road soon passing the cattle market on the left.

Continue through the suburbs of Melton with a shared-use cycle path available briefly on the left and right as far as the school. The traffic and houses are soon left behind and at the first junction **turn L**, signed for Holwell, onto

46

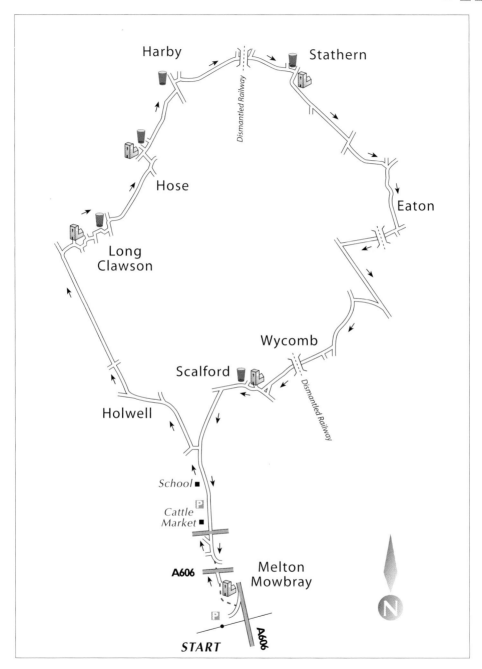

Harby

Stathern

Dismantled Railway

Hose

Eaton

Long
Clawson

Wycomb

Scalford

Holwell

Dismantled Railway

School ■

*Cattle
Market* ■

A606

Melton
Mowbray

N

START

A606

Holwell Lane. Bear right with the road at the next junction, cross a cattle grid and continue on towards Holwell at a further junction and cross another cattle grid to leave the underground mining danger zone.

Climb into Holwell and keep with the main road, heading for Long Clawson and ignoring minor turns. At a 'Give Way' at a crossroads go straight ahead, still heading for Long Clawson, with developing views across the valley below. A long gradual descent leads into Long Clawson, where follow the road as it twists and turns through the village heading for Hose all the while. In Hose continue with the main road, heading for Harby, or turn left for a pub stop.

At a 'Give Way' nearing Harby **turn L** and once in the village immediately **turn R**, for Stathern, onto Stathern Lane. Straight on at this junction leads to the pubs and filling station.

Pass under a railway bridge and then **turn R** for Stathern, where **turn R** at the 'Give Way'. Pass the Plough Inn and follow the road to the right heading for Eaton. Climb away from the village and shortly before the top of the hill **turn L**, signed for Eaton, and at a staggered junction **turn R** and then **L**, still heading for Eaton.

In Eaton **turn R**, signed 'gated road', for Waltham, ignoring the left hand Elm Lane. The road winds and undulates then climbs until

shortly beyond the top of the hill **turn R** heading for Eastwell. Another down and then up leads to a T-junction, where **turn L** and in approximately 1 mile **turn R**, signed for Goadby Marwood and Wycomb, followed by a **L turn** for Chadwell and Wycomb. At the next junction bear right with the road heading for Wycomb and Scalford, ignore the right turn into Wycomb village and continue on to Scalford. Follow the road to the right into the village and **turn L** onto Church Street, keeping the church on the right. **Turn L** at the next junction, which then leads back to Melton Mowbray via the outward route.

MELTON CARNEGIE MUSEUM
Melton Carnegie Museum is located at Thorpe End and houses displays on county sports, Melton stories and local industries such as pork pies. The museum is open Monday to Saturday from 10 am to 5 pm.

ST MARY'S CHURCH
St Mary's is renowned as the largest and stateliest parish church in Leicestershire and houses many fine examples of stained glass. It is open to the public all year from 10 am to 12 noon and 2 pm to 4 pm Monday to Saturday.

CATTLE MARKET
Melton Mowbray is indeed an ancient market town, with a record of market rights being granted as far back as 1077. This is considerably earlier than the majority of towns in Leicestershire and Rutland, 44 of which are recorded to have gained their market rights by 1350.

10

Burrough Hill and the Dalbys

18 miles

Burrough Hill is a magnificent viewpoint looking over the Wreake Valley below and away to Charnwood Forest in the distance, and a must to visit either before or after the ride. And when you are on the route, dipping and climbing in a circuit around the hill-fort, good views are never far away. Approximately half way round there is the opportunity to sample the product of one of the jewels in Leicestershire's crown, the still independent Everard's brewery. The Carrington Arms at Ashby Folville is a great example of the English country pub, and on a summer's day with a pint of Tiger and the sounds of village cricket wafting across the road time really does stand still.

Maps: OS Landranger 129 and 141

Starting point: Burrough Hill Country Park pay-and-display car park. GR 766115

By train: From Melton Mowbray the route can be joined at Great Dalby in approximately 3 miles via minor roads and the B6047.

Refreshments: There are toilets and a pleasant picnic area at Burrough Hill, but no other facilities. There are pubs in several of the villages along the way, and the Carrington Arms in Ashby Folville is highly recommended: it is pleasantly situated, has a garden and is open all day Saturday and Sunday. Food is generally available with rolls on offer when the main menu is not being served. The Carrington Arms is an Everard's pub, still thankfully a common feature in Leicestershire.

The route: A hilly circuit on mainly minor roads, but with some busier sections – a good choice for a family outing with older children once basic skills and traffic awareness have been learnt.

From the car park a track leads to Burrough Hill Iron Age hill-fort, a recommended diversion. There is no cycling access to the hill-fort itself and if the track is busy remember to give way to pedestrians. There are extensive views from the hill-fort, a trig point and toposcope. Leicestershire County Council owns the hilltop and allows open access. The best views are from the toposcope looking across the valley to Leicester and beyond.

Return through the car park and at the road junction **turn L** to arrive shortly in Somerby. Keep with the

The view from Burrough Hill across the Wreake valley

main road, passing the Stilton Cheese pub, the Old Brewery Inn and then the church on the right to reach a 'Give Way', where **turn L**, heading for Pickwell and Melton. Take care through the village as parked cars can make the road narrow.

Continue through Pickwell, keeping with the main road, and after leaving the village take the **first L**, signed for Little Dalby. Keep heading for Little Dalby, descending and ignoring a turn to the left, and at the next junction **turn L** to pass through the hamlet of Little Dalby.

The road then winds and undulates pleasantly, with views back to the hill-fort on the left, to arrive in

Great Dalby, where **turn L** at the 'Give Way', signed for the village centre and Burrough. Keep right with the road at the next junction, still heading for the village centre, and at the T-junction **turn R**, signed for Melton Mowbray. On the next bend, and by the war memorial, **turn L** onto Top End. At the next junction **turn L** onto Station Road signed for Gadesby and Leicester. Pass under a railway bridge and continue straight on at the crossroads, heading for Ashby Folville. Go straight on again at the next crossroads and at the 'Give Way' just over a small bridge **turn R**, heading for Barsby. Ashby Folville village and the Carrington Arms are to the left at this junction.

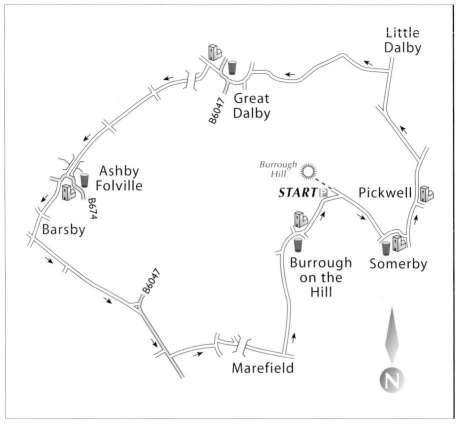

On the right-hand bend **turn L** to leave the main road, still heading for Barsby. In Barsby continue straight on at the crossroads and at the 'Give Way' **turn L**, heading for Twyford and Lowesby. Ignore a right-hand turn and arrive at a junction with the B6047, where **turn R** with care, heading for Tilton. Follow the B road for approximately 1 mile and shortly after a right turn for Hungerton take the minor road on the **L** signed for Marefield. At a junction by a cattle grid **turn L and shortly R**, again heading for Marefield.

Cross more cattle grids and pass under a disused railway, a further cattle grid, and so to Marefield.

A little way out of Marefield **turn L**, signed for Burrough; climb, descend and climb once more on the rough, pot-holed road to a T-junction, where **turn R** still heading for Burrough. In Burrough on the Hill **keep R** with the road, passing the Stag and Hounds, and then **turn L** with the road to climb back to Burrough Hill Country Park on the left at the top of the hill.

The ancient earthworks at Burrough Hill

BURROUGH HILL COUNTRY PARK

The park contains a large hill-fort which may have been the pre-Roman capital of the local tribe, the Coritani. The country parks service of Leicestershire County Council runs a series of events throughout the year such as an Iron Age hill-fort guided walk and autumn wildlife and nocturnal creatures guided walks.

BURROUGH HOUSE AND BOWER HOUSE

In the village of Burrough on the Hill are two late 19th- early 20th-century houses which were once used as hunting boxes. Burrough Hall, to the Northeast of the village, and Burrough House, near the lane to Owston. The gardens of the latter feature a Bower House where Edward, Prince of Wales was said to have met Mrs Simpson in the 1930s.

THE LEICESTERSHIRE ROUND

The Leicestershire Round, which passes through Burrough Hill Country Park, is a 100 mile long distance footpath devised in 1987 for the centenary of the Leicestershire Footpath Association, using mainly footpaths and bridleways. The walk starts from Willoughby Waterleys, passes through Bradgate Park and finishes in Frisby.

EVERARD'S

Everard's brewery was founded in 1849 in Leicester when William Everard of Narborough joined forces with a local maltster, Thomas Hull. The operation grew to serve many local pubs and also purchased and ran its own houses, which now number 150 and include hotels and restaurants. The company remains family owned.

Market Harborough and the Brampton Valley Way

22 miles

The creation of the National Cycle Network over recent years has been a boon for cyclists, with many new routes created, the best parts of which are often along disused railway lines. The Brampton Valley Way is just such an example, and one of the highlights of the network nationally as well as locally, linking Northampton with Market Harborough on National Route 6. It is also one of the highlights of this route, complete with its two very dark tunnels, but there is also plenty more to see along the way, including the beautiful estate village of Cottesbrooke with its hall and gardens, and Naseby of battlefield fame.

Map: OS Landranger 141

Starting point: Market Harborough Market Hall car park by the bus station. GR 735870. Note – there is free parking in all the town centre car parks.

By train: Market Harborough is on the Midland Mainline railway line.

Refreshments: Market Harborough has many shops, pubs, cafés and restaurants. There are few other facilities on the route but there are pubs in Maidwell, Clipston and Naseby, where the Fitzgerald Arms is recommended. It features information on the battle of Naseby, serves excellent home-cooked food and has a pleasant outdoor area.

The route: A long but largely level, traffic-free route, but care is needed in Market Harborough, on the two A508 crossings, and on the busier road between Naseby and Clipston. The off-road section on the Brampton Valley Way is good all year, but the track beyond Blueberry Lodge may be muddy in winter. Sustrans' National Cycle Network Route 6 goes through the centre of Market Harborough and is well signed throughout, heading south for the Brampton Valley Way. Although the full ride would be too much for small children, or as a first trip, out and back excursions along the Brampton Valley Way are a great introduction to cycling. Start either in Harborough or from the parking near Maidwell, but remember those tunnels – kids will either love them or hate them, so be prepared. While it is possible to brave the dark and walk, lights are recommended.

Kelmarsh tunnel on the Brampton Valley Way

From the Market Hall car park **turn L** and follow the cycleway alongside the A508. Go straight on at the traffic lights and then **turn L** onto Aulreca Street, signed for NCN route 6 throughout. **Turn R** at the end of the street onto a tarmac cyclepath which follows the edge of the park. Pass a millennium milepost by the Bell public house and continue to a road crossing, where cross with care onto the Brampton Valley Way.

The Way passes first through Oxendon tunnel, 418 metres, and then Kelmarsh tunnel, 480 metres. Note the warnings: both are very dark and lights are recommended. It is generally better to walk, but don't be put off – the way through is straight and you can always see the light at the end of the tunnel!

Follow the Brampton Valley Way for approximately 6 miles to Draughton car park, where **turn R** at the road crossing, heading for Maidwell village. Wind through the village of Maidwell, passing the church and school to the A508, where **turn R** and immediately **L with care** onto the 'no through road'. Keep with the road, passing on the left Dale Farm. The road becomes rough and pot-holed before arriving at Blueberry Lodge, where continue straight ahead, signed for Cottesbrooke. Beyond the lodge the route is at first rough track, then field edge, before improving back to tarmac at a

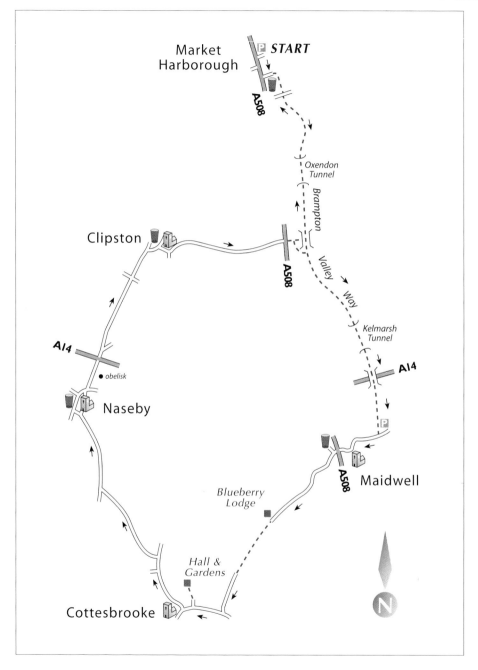

A novel waymark guides the cyclist

small plantation. It is then followed to a junction by farm buildings, passing a view to the right of Cottesbrooke Hall. **Turn R** into the picturesque estate village of Cottesbrooke where a minor road to the right gives access to the hall and gardens.

Continue to a junction, where **turn R**, signed for Haselbech and Naseby, pass the church on the left and continue out of the village and into open parkland. **Keep R** at a minor junction signed for Naseby, and take the **next L** at another minor unsigned junction, passing through a white gate. At the next junction **turn R** and climb to arrive

in Naseby by the Naseby Battle and Farm Museum.

Continue on through the village, heading for Clipston. At the T-junction with Church Street **turn R**, pass the Royal Oak on the left and then the church and Fitzgerald Arms, all the while still heading for Clipston. **Keep L** on leaving the village and in ½ mile arrive at the obelisk commemorating the Battle of Naseby. Continue, taking care as there can be occasional fast vehicles, cross the new A14, and in a little way go straight on at a crossroads and into Clipston.

Keep with the road to the right and by the Old Red Lion pub (with pleasant outside eating area) **turn R**, signed for Kelmarsh. By the church **keep L** – signed for Great Oxendon and Arthingworth. Continue now on the quieter by-road to the A508. Cross **with great care** onto a small track that is followed to a junction with the Brampton Valley Way by a bridge. Rejoin the cycle way **turning L** to return to Market Harborough via the Oxendon tunnel.

• •

BRAMPTON VALLEY WAY

This delightful 14-mile-long Sustrans route starts from Little Barden crossing, Market Harborough and continues through rolling countryside to Broughton crossing, Northamptonshire, following the track bed of a disused railway. As such the route is flat and therefore easy apart from negotiating its two long dark tunnels, where extra lighting is definitely needed!

BLUEBERRY LODGE
Blueberry Lodge is a project of the Hawk and Owl Trust, a long-term study of owls and other birds of prey.

COTTESBROOKE HALL
The hall and gardens are open from Easter to the end of September. Both are open 2 pm–5.30 pm. Thursday afternoons, bank holiday Sundays and Mondays, otherwise the first Sunday of each month. Gardens only are open 2 pm–5.30 pm, Tuesday, Wednesday and Friday from May.

NASEBY BATTLE AND FARM MUSEUM
The museum is open from Easter till September on bank holiday Sundays and Mondays from 2 pm–5 pm. At other times for parties by arrangement.

BATTLE OF NASEBY
The Battle of Naseby took place between the third week in May and 14th June 1645. It resulted in a distinctive loss for the Royalists who had almost 1,000 killed and 4,500 captured, compared with Parliament losses of 200 men on the field. King Charles I also lost his baggage train, his private papers and effectively his throne. The battlefield itself has changed little since the 17th century, with a monument erected by the Cromwell

The obelisk commemorating the Battle of Naseby

Association marking the approximate position of Cromwell's squadron at the start of the battle. The obelisk placed in 1825 is about 1 mile from where the action took place and was erected by John and Mary Frances Fitzgerald, Lord and Lady of the Manor of Naseby.

The Langtons and the Grand Union Canal

18 miles

When the National Cycle Network's off-road highlights aren't following disused railways (see route 11) they are often along canal towpaths. This route includes just such a delightful section of National Route 6 along the Grand Union Canal between Debdale Wharf and Market Harborough via the popular Foxton Locks. Away from the canal the route passes through Thorpe Langton, Church Langton and Tur Langton, all with notable churches. However, it was at Church Langton in 1759 that the first rendition of Handel's *Messiah* in a parish church took place – a notable first!

Map: OS Landranger 141

Starting point: Kibworth Beauchamp – Pagett Street car park, which is just off the roundabout near the centre of the village. GR 683937

By train: From Market Harborough, where the route can be joined at Great Bowden via a minor road in 1 mile.

Refreshments: Kibworth Beauchamp has several pubs, shops, and restaurants and Great Bowden is on the outskirts of Market Harborough, which has all the facilities you'd expect of a busy market town. There are also several pubs and other refreshment points passed on the route, including a shop, tearoom and pub at Foxton Locks. Note that as in many rural areas pubs may not be open at lunchtime during the week, an example being the Bakers Arms in Thorpe Langton. It does, however, serve lunch at weekends between 12 noon and 2 pm, and food in the evenings between 6.30 pm and 9.30 pm.

The route: There are a few hills and a lot of off-road but this is a moderately easy route for the distance. The off-road towpath was recently repaired and is good all year, but the track from Smeeton Westerby to Debdale Wharf is across open fields which may be muddy in places during wet weather. There are a few busy road crossings, but the majority of the route is lightly used by vehicles and the road from Great Bowden to Welham is no longer a vehicular through route.

Turn R out of the car park to return to the roundabout, where **turn R** for Fleckney. Shortly afterwards take the **first L** on Smeeton Road, signed for Smeeton Westerby. Continue into Smeeton

The Bottom Lock at Foxton Locks

Westerby and just before the phone box on the right **turn L** onto Debdale Lane. Follow this lane, which becomes a track through open fields, to Debdale Wharf.

At Debdale Wharf **turn R** at the minor road and at the bridge over the Grand Union Canal **turn R** before crossing to join the canal towpath. Follow the towpath to the left, which leads to Foxton Locks at the junction of the Grand Union Canal and its spur that runs to Market Harborough. Crossing the bridge over the canal here accesses the café, shop, pub and boat trips; our route, however, continues on the same bank to follow the spur.

Cross a minor road at Foxton swing bridge, continuing along the towpath which now becomes National Cycle Network Route 6. Pass a millennium milepost where the towpath passes under the B6047 and at Bowden Hall Bridge leave the canal side and Route 6. **Turn L** at the road, heading towards Great Bowden, where continue into the village, cross the railway bridge and pass the Red Lion pub before **turning R** and then **L** by the village green and the Shoulder of Mutton. **Turn L** again just before the church, **bear R** with the road and then **turn L** onto Welham Lane, marked 'Unsuitable for Motors' and signed as a dead end. Cross the narrow bridge that makes this a no through road for vehicles and continue on to Welham, where **turn L**.

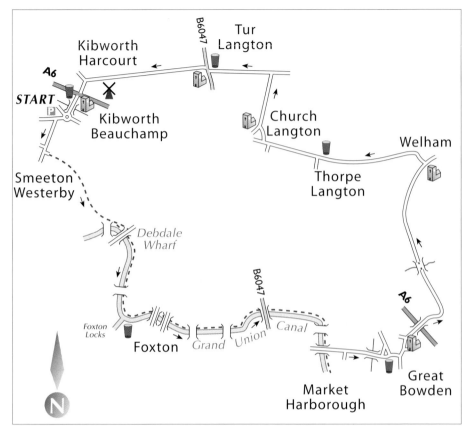

Pass through Thorpe Langton and by the Bakers Arms and after passing a left turn for East Langton **turn R** onto Church Causeway for Church Langton. At the junction in front of the church **turn R** to descend and at a T-junction **turn L** heading for Tur Langton. At the 'Give Way' in Tur Langton **turn R** and immediately **L** by the Bull's Head, heading for Kibworth.

Turn L in Kibworth Harcourt onto Marsh Drive, signed for Kibworth Beauchamp, and at the junction with the A6 **turn R with care** and immediately **L** by the Coach and Horses to return to the roundabout and car parking.

• •

FOXTON LOCKS

Built in 1812, this staircase of ten locks rises 75ft to reach the summit. This is also the site of the Foxton Inclined Plane, an ingenious design to raise boats up the slope and by – pass the locks. Built in 1900, this however, proved an unpopular alternative and closed in 1911. A leaflet *Exploring the Grand Union Canal* can be obtained from the Tourist Information Centre. The locks attract a number of people as there are many other facilities to be found here. Horse-drawn-barge trips are available in season, also boat services, canal information and daily boat hire. There is also a pub selling food, a canal side garden, tearooms and shop.

GREAT BOWDEN
Great Bowden's 13th-century church, which is topped by a 14th-century spire, once claimed the whole of Market Harborough in its parish. The church was still using its graveyard facilities for the entire parish long after the foundation of Market Harborough in the parish of Great Bowden at the end of the 12th century.

TUR LANGTON
At some stage during his flight after his defeat at the Battle of Naseby, Charles I visited Tur Langton, where he watered his horse at what is still known as King Charles' Well. At one time this was the only source of water in the area and did not run dry even during the drought of 1976.

A millennium milepost on the route

Burbage Common and the Soar Valley

18 miles

A route of contrasts, with surprisingly rural sections juxtaposed with the busy settlements you'd expect so close to the outskirts of Hinckley and Leicester. Quiet lanes cross busy main roads, and the modern M69 parallels the route of the Roman Fosse Way. The popular Burbage Common and Woods serves as our start and finish for this circuit of villages in the Soar Valley.

Map: OS Landranger 140

Starting point: Burbage Common and Woods, at Smithy Lane, just off the A5070. There is parking along the lane and at its end, by a bridleway signed for Burbage Common and Woods. GR 451946

By train: From Hinckley, where the route is best joined at Aston Flamville on minor roads via Burbage in approximately 3 miles.

Refreshments: Broughton Astley is a large village with shops and pubs including Everard's Ye Old Bull's Head offering lunchtime food. There are many other pubs and occasional shops in the villages *en route*, of note being the Queen's Arms in Leire, with a pleasant outside seating area, and the Heathcote Arms in Croft at the bottom of Croft Hill – another Everard's pub.

The route: The absence of steep hills makes this a moderately easy ride, but busy roads are encountered in several places necessitating care. The bridleway across Burbage Common is mainly broad and grassy, but a couple of rocky and muddy areas may be slippery in winter.

Return along Smithy Lane to the A5070, where **turn R with care** and then shortly **turn L** just after the sign for Burbage, signed for Aston Flamville and Sharnford. There is a pavement on the right-hand side of the A5070.

Cross over the motorway and continue into Aston Flamville, pass the church and thatched cottages,

and carry on through the village to Sharnford. **Turn L** with the one way system, joining the B4114, which is followed past the Countryman and the Sharnford Arms pubs to climb out of the village with the church on the right. Shortly **turn R with care**, signed for Frolesworth, Leire, Ashby Parva and Fosse Meadows.

The broad grassy track across Burbage Common

At a crossroads with the Fosse Way Roman road, straight on leads to Frolesworth and right leads to the Fosse Meadows nature reserve, which is accessed via a parking area signed for the picnic site and nature trails.

After visiting the nature reserve continue into Frolesworth, passing the church on the right and keeping with the main road through the village, heading for Leire. In Leire **turn L**, signed for Broughton and Cosby by the Queen's Arms and the church. Continue under a railway bridge and follow the pleasantly winding road to a junction where **turn R**.

In Broughton Astley **turn L** at the

'Give Way' by Ye Old Bull's Head and continue through the village, passing shops and a garage, to arrive at a junction with the busy B581. **Turn L** signed for Stoney Stanton, and almost immediately **turn R with care**, signed 'Sutton Elms Only'. The road ends at a turning circle, where continue straight on through the gate on the old road leading towards the B4114. **Turn R** on the shared-use cycle and footpath before reaching the busy dual carriageway. This leads past a signed 'unsuitable crossing place' to a point opposite the road to Croft; dismount here and **cross with care** and follow the minor road into Croft.

Keep with the main road through

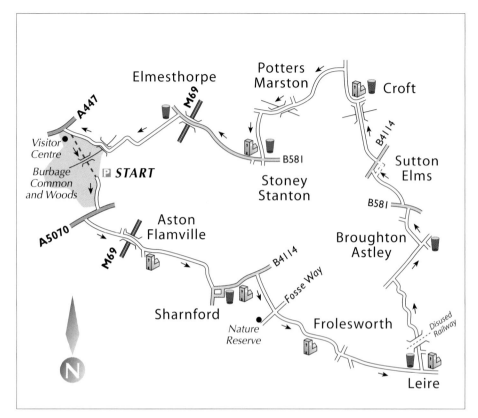

the village, cross the railway bridge and **turn L** in front of the Heathcote Arms. Climb, passing the church on the right, and at the top of the hill **turn L** onto Stanton Lane, signed for Potters Marston, Stoney Stanton and Sapcote. Continue through Potters Marston, ignoring a right turn to cross the railway and then keeping with the road on a sharp left bend to enter Stoney Stanton. Pass the Francis Arms and the Blue Bell pubs and at a 'Stop' sign **turn R with care** onto the B581. Continue through the village by more pubs, shops and the church. **Keep R** at a mini-

roundabout, still on the B581 and heading for Elmesthorpe. In Elmesthorpe cross the motorway bridge and **turn L** by the telephone box and just before the pub onto Burbage Common Road.

Follow the narrow lane, crossing the railway, to eventually arrive at Burbage Common Visitor Centre, where **turn L** into the car park. Follow the bridleway to the left of the Visitor Centre onto the common, almost doubling back on the road just followed. The bridleway continues as a broad grassy track across the common and is marked by posts with a blue flash. Pass under a railway bridge on a stony track and continue in the same direction, still following the bridleway, to **turn L** at a junction with a surfaced track. This leads via a gate back onto Smithy Lane.

● ●

BURBAGE COMMON VISITOR CENTRE

The Visitor Centre houses an exhibition, information, small shop and toilets. Opening times vary according to the time of year, but the centre can usually be found to be open on weekend afternoons.

FOSSE WAY

The word 'fosse' is thought to derive from 'fossa' meaning 'ditch'. The Fosse Way, which runs from Lincoln to Axmouth, has a ditch on either side (as did all Roman roads). Originally it was referred to as Fosse and then Fosse Street, finally being known as the Fosse Way in the 15th century.

FOSSE MEADOWS NATURE RESERVE

This reserve comprises mainly meadowland. A meadow trail – a 20-minute walk – explains why hay meadows have almost disappeared and shows how evidence of past use can be found by close observation of the landscape. A 35-minute walk down a woodland trail marked with red arrows has boards explaining why different types of woodland were planted here. Note that although these trails are marked with blue and red arrows, normally the indicators of bridleways and byways respectively, these are in fact only rights of way on foot. Cycle racks are available near the portaloo.

MILL ON THE SOAR

Just off route near Sutton Elms at the junction of the B581 and B4114 is the Mill on the Soar. This houses a falconry centre that gives flying demonstrations with owls, hawks, falcons and buzzards; there is also a fishing lake. Open from April to the end of September daily between 11 am and 5 pm. It is closed on Mondays and Tuesdays for the rest of the year. There is also an Everard's hotel and function suite with the same name that is built around the historic water mill and set in extensive grounds overlooking the fishing lake.

Quiet lanes and windmills south of Leicester

13 miles

The ancient Guthlaxton Hundred, within which this route falls and which gives its name to the Guthlaxton Cycle Trail briefly followed, has its origin in the Danelaw, but the name is old English. This meeting place by a stone, most likely Guthlac's stone, grew to become an important public meeting place under the Danelaw. The pretty villages encountered on the ride also reflect these mixed origins, with Bruntingthorpe and Arnesby being derived from old Danish, but Gilmorton, Kimcote, Walton and Peatling from old English. In this area with a rich Roman past you may be forgiven for thinking the Parva and Magna affixes relate to those times, but they are actually medieval additions made by clerks working in Latin which eventually supplanted the vernacular Little and Great. Place names aside, there are few popular attractions on this ride, the peace that brings being part of the appeal, but do look out for the windmills in Arnesby and Gilmorton.

Map: OS Landranger 140

Starting point: Gilmorton. There is on-road parking in Gilmorton and also a small parking area next to the recreation ground and tennis court just beyond the Talbot pub, from where the route is described. GR 573877

By train: No convenient rail start.

Refreshments: There are pubs in several villages along the route, the most convenient for a break on the way being The Plough at Bruntingthorpe, which is open all day Saturday and Sunday, and the Old Cock Inn at Arnesby, which has a pleasant outdoor seating area.

The route: A relatively short and easy circuit just to the south of Leicester. With few nearby tourist attractions, and only small villages *en route*, these roads are generally quiet and so this makes a good introductory family ride once basic bike skills and traffic awareness have been learnt.

From the recreation ground follow Lutterworth Road towards the village centre, passing the Talbot pub on the left. At a junction by the Crown **turn R**, heading for Kimcote.

At the 'Give Way' in Kimcote **turn**

The windmill at Arnesbury

L, heading for Walton and Harborough. In Walton keep with the main road, heading for Bruntingthorpe, ignoring a left turn also signed for Bruntingthorpe. The road leads eventually to a T-junction where **turn L**, again heading for Bruntingthorpe, and pass the entrance to Bruntingthorpe, Aerodrome and Proving Ground.

Pass through Bruntingthorpe, by the Plough and keeping with the road as it winds through the village. After approximately 1 mile **turn R**, signed for Arnesby, and **keep R** at the next junction with the Guthlaxton Trail, part of National Cycle Network Route 6, which will be followed after visiting the village of Arnesby.

Note the now private mill on the left and the Old Cock Inn on the right, before returning to the junction mentioned above, where **turn R**, signed as a gated road for Peatling Magna and the Guthlaxton Trail. Pass through two gates and follow the road as it winds pleasantly into Peatling Magna, **turn L** by the Old Cock Inn, heading for Gilmorton.

Continue straight on at the crossroads and in Peatling Parva, after passing the church and Shires Free House, **turn L** by the triangle and tree planted to commemorate the diamond jubilee of Queen Victoria and shortly after **turn R** at

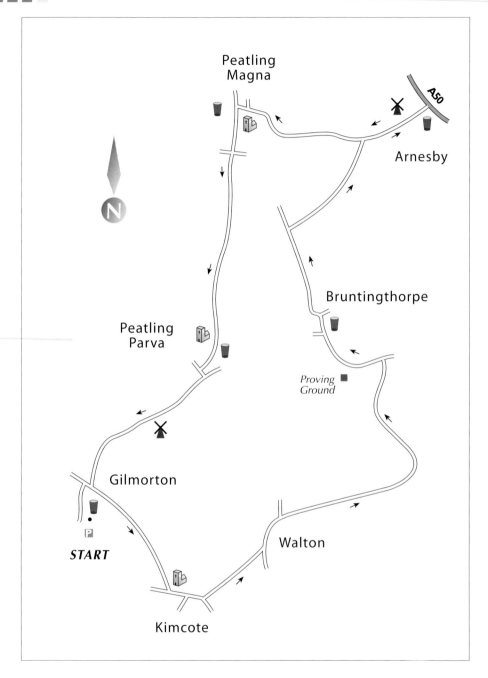

Peatling Magna

Arnesby

A50

N

Bruntingthorpe

Peatling Parva

Proving Ground

Gilmorton

START

Walton

Kimcote

the next junction, heading for Gilmorton.

Pass a recently converted windmill on the left and at the junction by the Crown in Gilmorton **turn R** and then **L** to return to the parking by the tennis courts.

● ●

ARNESBY WINDMILL
A brick tower mill built in 1815 on the site of a former post mill, Arnesby windmill served the village from 1653. It has now been converted into a private dwelling

GILMORTON WINDMILL
This 19th-century former windmill has now been converted into a unique dwelling.

BRUNTINGTHORPE AERODROME AND PROVING GROUND
A former RAF station and USAF base, Bruntinghtorpe was bought in 1983 by C Walton Ltd. It now provides a home for a large collection of historic aircraft, including the world's last flying Comet and two Lightnings. It is also used by vehicle and component manufacturers for its high-speed-track test facilities.

The Guthlaxton Trail waymarks

GUTHLAXTON CYCLE TRAIL
This trail is part of the National Cycle Network Route 6, which runs from Derby to Oxford.

Out and about in Charnwood Forest

16 miles

A route packed with attractions around the ancient hunting forest of Charnwood and the highest ground in Leicestershire. The viewpoints of Old John Tower and Beacon Hill combine with ancient woodlands and the picturesque Swithland Reservoir – magnificently crossed by the Great Central steam railway – to make a ride to savour.

Map: OS Landranger 129

Starting point: Quorn, on National Cycle Network Route 6, where there is free parking in the town centre on Station Road by the Medical Centre. GR 562165

By train: Quorn and Woodhouse Station on the Great Central Railway, which runs from Loughborough to Leicester. This is the UK's only double-track Heritage railway and combines with the cycle ride to make a great day out. Trains, including steam, run daily throughout the summer and in winter on weekends and bank holidays. The timetable is subject to change so please check before travelling.

Refreshments: There are many restaurants and pubs in Quorn, the Quorndon Fox being of particular note as it is open all day for food and families are welcome. It is an interesting, large, old country house and has a garden at the rear. *En route* there are pubs in Swithland and Woodhouse Eaves but few other facilities.

The route: Although relatively short in distance, the route includes several strenuous hills and off-road sections, making it a moderately hard outing. The off-road track around Swithland reservoir is largely on a good surface, but the bridleway through Swithland Wood may be muddy in places.

Follow Station Road towards the town centre and **turn L** by the Royal Oak, following National Cycleway Route 6 towards Leicester and Mountsorrel. Shortly after passing the Quorn Country House Hotel on the left, **turn R** signed for Swithland, and climb up and past the Mountsorrel Quarry.

Ignore minor junctions until reaching a crossroads in Rothley, where **turn R**, still heading for Swithland. Pass under the Great Central Railway and then over the beautiful Swithland Reservoir before arriving in Swithland by the Swithland Spring Water Company.

A parkland view from the Swithland reservoir dam

Keep with the main road through the village, heading for Woodhouse Eaves, and after a short climb **turn L** at a T-junction signed for Roecliffe Manor, Newton Linford and Bradgate Country Park. Continue climbing, passing car parks for Bradgate Country Park and Swithland Wood North, and immediately after a left bend **turn L** onto a rough bridle track which soon turns to tarmac.

After an area of caravans, and where the track turns to the right and climbs, go straight on into the woods. Stick to the broad track as it bends to the left and climb slightly ignoring cycle tracks on the left coming from below. After passing spoil heaps above to the right the track descends, followed by a brief climb with open fields to the left leading to a gate at the car park and road.

Turn R at the road and climb to Roecliffe crossroads, with views of the Old John Tower to the left. Note that a path runs along the right-hand side of the road and can be reached via the road through the car park, so avoiding this fairly busy section of road. **Turn L** at the crossroads and continue climbing to a junction at the top of the hill. On the left is Hunts Hill car park at the head of which is a broad track that leads to the viewpoint of the Old John Tower. Cycling is not permitted along this track, so please walk with your bike.

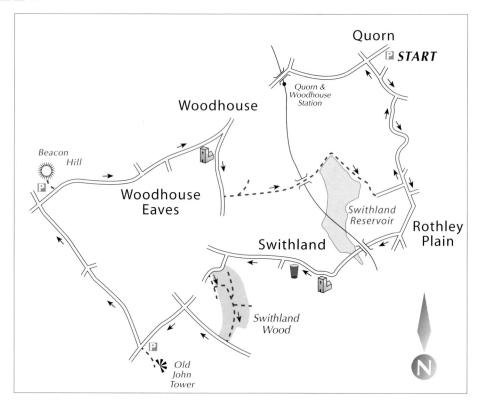

After visiting the viewpoint return to the junction on the bend and take the minor road heading for Shepshed. Continue straight on at the first crossroads and **turn R** at the second, Beacon Hill crossroads, signed for Woodhouse Eaves.

At the top of the hill on the left the car park leads to Beacon Hill Country Park, Beacon Hill being the second highest point in Leicestershire, where there are maps, an information board and toilets. A tarmac road leads through the upper car park, almost to the summit, which is surprisingly wild and rocky. Take note of the 'no cycling' signs and walk as appropriate.

After visiting the summit return to the road and make a rapid descent **with care** through Woodhouse Eaves to Woodhouse. By the church **turn R** very sharply onto School Lane, which is followed for approximately ¾ mile then **turn L** onto a minor lane signed as 'unsuitable for motors'. **Keep R** at a fork by Rushey Fields Farm and continue on the track to cross over the railway line just before Swithland Reservoir.

The track then follows the

northern shore before climbing away from the reservoir to a junction, where **turn L** to return towards Quorn, passing the quarry seen on the outward journey. At the mini-roundabout **turn L** and so back to the centre of Quorn, where **turn R** for the car park.

●●●●●●●●●●●●●●●●●●●●●●●

MOUNTSORREL QUARRY

With its grey and pink granite intrusion Mountsorrel Quarry is illustrative of the final phase in the emplacement of the rocks that make up Charnwood Forest, which occurred some 400 million years ago in Silurian times.

GREAT CENTRAL RAILWAY

This is Britain's only double-track, main line steam railway. There are main line steam train rides every weekend and bank holiday throughout the year, and daily from May until September. This special railway has the added attraction of serving a four-or six-course meal at select times while enjoying the journey.

OLD JOHN TOWER

Old John Tower is probably the best-known landmark in the area, situated 700 feet above sea level and with extensive views around the county. It is a stone crenellated tower, which was built around 1784 by the 5th Earl of Stamford.

BEACON HILL

Beacon Hill is one of Leicestershire's most visited viewpoints and is found on the edge of Charnwood Forest. The hill's summit is ringed with the faint traces of a rampart that has been associated with the Iron Age. The discovery of a Bronze Age hoard suggests that the occupation of the hilltop, and possibly the hill-fort itself, may well date back to before the Iron Age.

SWITHLAND RESERVOIR

This is a popular site with the Leicester and Rutland Ornithological Society as many examples of winter wildfowl can be seen, as well as freshwater and sea duck species, in addition to a large selection of other birds. It is especially known for being the most reliable site in Leicestershire to see peregrines in the winter.

QUORN

Quorn should really be known as Quorndon, and derives from 'cweorn', the Saxon word for 'millstone'. The suffix comes from 'dun', meaning hill. The name hasn't changed a great deal over time, in 1209 it was Querendon and in the 13th century, Querondon. Hugh Meynell, who founded the famous Quorn Hunt, lived at Quorndon Hall.

Family trails in Bradgate Park and Swithland Woods

7 miles

The impressive Bradgate Park has long been a popular resort for the people of Leicester, ever since it was donated for their 'quiet recreation' by a local businessman in 1928. This route is in fact two short 'out and back' excursions from the Hallgates car park, one on-road through the Park, and the other off-road in the more secluded Swithland Woods. Only a very small amount of public road is encountered, making these ideal introductory rides in beautiful surroundings.

Maps: OS Landranger 129 and 140

Starting point: Hallgates car park, Bradgate Park. GR 542114

By train: Quorn and Woodhouse station, see route 15.

Refreshments: There is a shop and teashop at the Newton Linford end of Bradgate Park.

The route: In Bradgate Park cycling is permitted on the tarmac carriageway only, and cyclists should ride slowly, and carefully and give way to pedestrians. At busy times, particularly weekends and bank holidays, cycling is not permitted – except for small accompanied children. However, at quiet times, such as a grey weekday afternoon this is an ideal place for children and adults learning to cycle. The off-road route in Swithland Woods may be muddy in places, but is a great introduction to off-road cycling. As ever when riding off-road take care and always give way to walkers.

On-road through Bradgate Park (4 miles):
Go through the gate from Hallgates car park into Bradgate Park. A tarmac road leads via the old packhorse bridge and remains of Bradgate House to the car park at the Newton Lindford end with a gift shop, teashop, toilets and

nearby Bradgate Garden Centre. The return route is back along the same road.

Off-road loop of Swithland Woods (3 miles):
Turn L on the road out of Hallgates car park, climb and in a little way **turn R with care**, marked as a

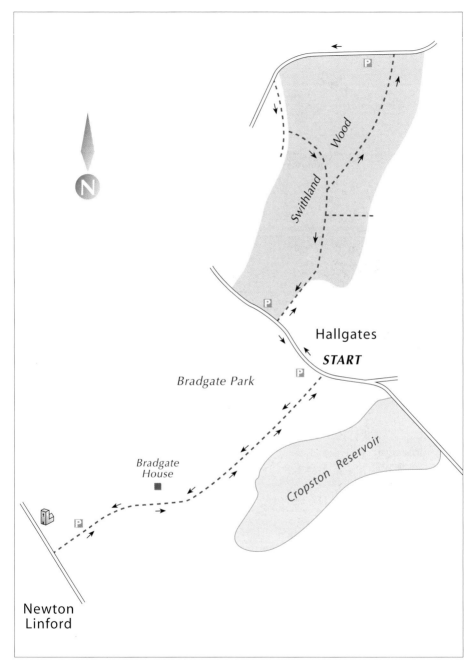

bridle road for Swithland Wood
and the car park. Follow the bridle
road into the wood, marked by
yellow slashes on wooden posts.

Historic Bradgate Park

After 500m ignore a marked trail going 90 degrees to the right, and shortly **fork R** at a further junction to descend, keeping with the broad track, which eventually narrows. **Keep L** at a muddy junction where the route ahead is not obvious; a yellow slash marker at the top of the rise marks the way and the track continues now quite narrow.

At the next possibly confusing junction by a yellow slash post **keep R** to arrive at the road by a car park. **Turn L** and climb on-road until just after a sharp left-hand bend, where **turn L** onto a rough bridle track which soon turns to tarmac.

After an area of caravans, and where the track turns to the right and climbs, go straight on into the woods.

Stick to the broad track as it bends to the left and climb slightly, ignoring cycle tracks on the left coming from below. After passing spoil heaps above to the right the track descends, followed by a brief climb with open fields to the left leading to a gate at the car park and road. **Turn L** to return to Hallgates car park.

● ●

BRADGATE PARK AND VISITOR CENTRE

This 850-acre medieval deer park first appears in documents around 1247 and contains the ruins of Bradgate House, which was built in 1500 and the birthplace of Lady Jane Grey. It is the largest country park in Leicestershire and is home to some of the oldest oak trees in the county. The park is open from dawn to dusk every day and has a pay and display car park at either end.

The Cloud Trail and The Trent Valley from Worthington

21 miles

The Sustrans National Cycle Network once again features prominently in this route, which incorporates an 8-mile off-road section of the Cloud Trail along the line of a disused railway which is a delight to cycle. At Swarkestone Lock on the Trent and Mersey Canal there is the option to explore the Cloud Trail further with a detour into Derby, but make sure you save enough time to enjoy the homeward leg, which has many attractions to explore. There is the ancient Swarkestone Bridge over the Trent flood plain, the stately Melbourne Hall, Breedon church perched on top of its conspicuous hill and a visit to the viewpoint over Staunton Harold Reservoir at Calke, all of which are too good to rush by.

Map: OS Explorer 245

Starting point: In the village of Worthington follow the signs for the Cloud Trail marked with a bicycle. This leads to a small amount of parking beyond the Station House. GR 407209

By train: Derby, joining the route at Swarkestone Lock via National Cycle Network Route 6.

Refreshments: The first refreshment stop *en route* is in Swarkestone at the Crewe and Harpur Arms, which is open all day every day for food and drink. It is located by the picturesque Swarkestone Bridge and has a river-fronted garden complete with a memorial cairn but is somewhat spoilt by the traffic. There are also several pubs and shops in Melbourne, and a café at Melbourne Hall.

The route: Although the Cloud Trail section is, of course, flat, there are several hills on the remainder of the route making it a moderately hard ride. A couple of busy roads are used, requiring care, especially the A514 over Swarkestone Bridge. The off-road along the Cloud Trail is good all year, but the byway from Stanton by Bridge to Melbourne may be muddy in places in winter. National Cycle Network Route 6, which incorporates the Cloud Trail, continues from Swarkestone Lock right into the heart of Derby and the rail station. This follows a level and largely traffic-free route and offers an interesting extension, or alternative rail start, but makes for a much longer outing, adding 10 miles.

The Trent and Mersey Canal

From the parking continue along the track, going straight ahead at the junction with National Cycle Network Route 6. Continue to a bridge, where follow the NCN Route 6 sign away from the valley to cross the busy A42 by a minor road and then rejoin the cycle trail via a track on the right.

The Cloud Trail now follows the line of the old railway (1887–1982), leading in 7½ miles to the Trent Viaduct and Sarson's Bridge over the Trent and Mersey canal, with views over the meadows and valley. The track now narrows and joins a minor road – take care with children on the narrow tarmac section just before the road.

Follow the road to the left, with views to the remains of Swarkestone Old Hall with its twin turrets and the church beyond. At the busy A514 follow the instructions on the sign, dismount, follow the footway round to the left and join the canal side directly from the footpath on the left-hand side. The canal towpath leads shortly to Swarkestone Lock and Swarkestone Junction, which is the junction of the Trent and Mersey and now disused Derby canals. A right turn here, following the signs for NCN Route 6, leads to Derby via off-road cycleway and shared-use cycle paths.

To continue on the route **turn L** on the rough road and pass under a

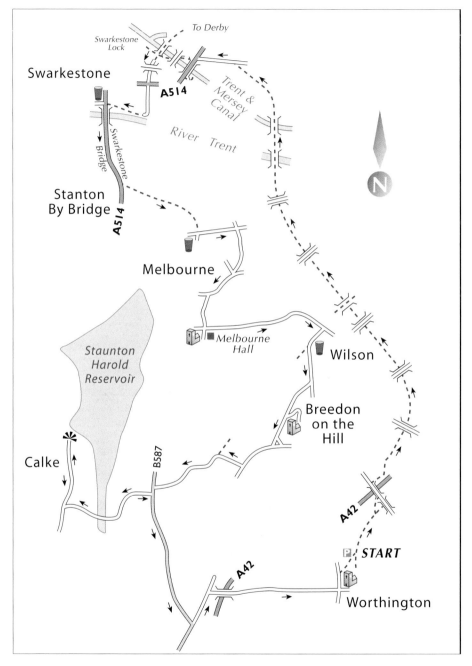

The village of Wilson visited on the ride

railway bridge to a junction with the A514. Cross with care onto Church Lane, which is followed as it turns right onto the river frontage. Keep with the lane and then path (dismount) to arrive at the road opposite the Crewe and Harpur Arms.

Turn L with care onto the A514 and over the bridge to continue across the ancient monument of Swarkestone Causeway. This is a busy road and although traffic speed tends to be restricted by the narrow passing points, great care is needed, especially with children.

At the other side of the causeway, immediately after the 40-mph speed limit sign, **turn L** onto the

minor road. This turns into a rough byway track that is followed as it climbs past Stanton Barn and then heads out between the open fields – the track is a little overgrown in places in summer, but generally good. Continue to a junction with the road by the Old Packhorse pub, where **turn L** at the mini-roundabout.

Follow the road now towards Kings Newton and at a junction by the war-memorial, where left leads back to the Cloud Trail, **turn R** onto Jawbone Lane. At the end of the lane **turn L** and immediately **R**, and at the junction by the green, **turn L** signed for Wilson and Breedon. Follow the road as it winds through the streets of

Melbourne to a T-junction in front of the church, Melbourne Hall and Gardens, Visitor Centre and craft shops, where **turn L**.

Note – the road passing the church and Visitor Centre leads to a private road by a lake and to the front of Melbourne Hall; free access when the gates are open.

Climb out of the village and on to Wilson, where a left turn offers a short cut back via the Cloud Trail. Keep with the road, heading for Breedon through the village, with views ahead to the church of Breedon on the Hill atop the quarried face. A little way out of Wilson **turn R** on a single-track road signed for Breedon Priory church. Climb to a junction where a **hairpin L** leads up to the church and viewpoint. Return to the junction and **turn L** to descend the other side of the hill into Breedon village.

Keep R in Breedon village and at the 'Give Way' **turn R**, heading out of the village. Pass a tearoom and craft centre on the right and then **turn R** onto a minor road. This leads in 1 mile to a junction with the B587 where **turn L** and almost immediately **R**, signed for Calke, to make a detour to the viewpoint over Staunton Harold reservoir.

Descend, cross the head of the reservoir and climb out the other side of the valley to a sharp left-hand bend, where **turn R** signed for Calke village only. This leads to a parking area with information boards and views across the reservoir and valley below.

Return through Calke and **turn L** to re-cross the valley back to the junction with the B587. **Turn R**, signed for Whitwick and Lount, and follow the B road for approximately 1½ miles, with views of Staunton Harold Hall below to the right, to a T-junction. **Turn L**, signed for Breedon and at the top of a small rise **turn R** with care. Cross the bridge over the busy A42 and return to Worthington, where **turn L** at the crossroads just before the church to return to the car park.

• •

THE CREWE AND HARPUR ARMS
The memorial cairn in the garden of the Crewe and Harpur Arms marks the furthest point south that was reached by the Jacobite army of Prince Charles Edward Stuart on 4 December 1745.

MELBOURNE HALL
Melbourne Hall was once the home of Victorian Prime Minister William Lamb, who as 2nd Viscount Melbourne gave his name to the city in Australia. The house is open every day in August between 2 pm and 4.15 pm except the first three Mondays. The Gardens are open from April to September between 1.30 pm and 5.30 pm, on Wednesdays, Saturdays, Sundays and bank holiday Mondays. There is a visitor centre which is open most days of the year and has a gift shop and estate workshops. The café is open every day from 11 am till 5 pm except Mondays (open bank holidays) and has a

Taking in the view over the River Trent

cyclists' welcome CTC sign in the window.

STAUNTON HAROLD RESERVOIR
This is a 200-acre reservoir and visitor centre with wild flower meadow, bird watching, dinghy and sail boarding. It was flooded in 1964.

SWARKESTONE BRIDGE
At almost one mile, Swarkestone Bridge is the longest stone bridge in England. It provides the area's major crossing point of the River Trent and it was here, in 1643, that the Battle of Swarkestone Bridge took place. Bonnie Prince Charlie's forces also reached the bridge in 1745 and then turned back, heading for Culloden.

Legend has it that the bridge was built early in the 13th century, on behalf of two beautiful sisters of the Bellamont family, in memory of their fiancés. During a joint betrothal party, the two men were summoned to a meeting on the other side of the Trent. In their haste to return to their beloved, the men braved re-crossing the river during a torrential storm and, subsequently, drowned. Neither girl every married and the ghosts of their fiancés are said to appear on stormy nights.

18

The Woulds Trail and the Ashby Canal

8 miles

A short, almost traffic-free, route steeped in the industrial heritage of the Midlands. This ride takes in a disused railway, restored canal, colliery transformed into a woodland park and a blast furnace converted to a museum and visitor centre. There are ample opportunities to stop for a picnic, or visit the Navigation Inn at the half-way point for refreshments and take a break in their large garden. All in all an excellent family day out.

Map: OS Explorer 245

Starting point: Measham – car parking by the library and public convenience. GR 332120.

By train: No convenient station.

Refreshments: There are cafés at Moira Furnace and the Conkers Centre. The Navigation Inn at Spring Cottage is open all day for food and drink.

The route: Following a disused railway and canal means no hills, and with an off-road surface that is good all year round this is an easy outing, ideal for families. There are a couple of road crossings where care is required, but otherwise this is a traffic-free ride.

From the car park follow the signs onto the Ashby Woulds Heritage Trail, signed Spring Cottage 3 miles. In approximately ½ mile join the footpath alongside the road to pass under the A42 and shortly rejoin the trail on the right.

The disused railway then continues via two bridges to a road by Donisthorpe church. Cross the road into Donisthorpe Woodland Park through the colourful gates, noting the information boards about the trail, colliery and routes through the park.

Continue to a track junction, where **turn R**, following the green waymarked 'Woodland Park Circular Route'. Pass a picnic area and old colliery wheel, keeping to the edge of the park throughout, and eventually arrive at the recently restored Ashby-de-la-Zouch Canal.

By a restored footbridge over the canal, and where the green waymarked route turns left, continue along the canal towpath to Moira Furnace. After visiting the furnace continue along the towpath to a junction with the B5003 by the fire station, cross with care and continue with the canal to the canal basin and Conkers Centre. From the head of the car park follow the track to the right of the playground fence and just before the bridge **turn L**, crossing the miniature railway, to rejoin the Heritage Trail, signed 3 miles to Measham.

Pass under a bridge and around a field edge and on entering woodland **turn R**, signed for Spring Cottage on an overgrown path. At the next junction by a small pond **turn R**, still heading for Spring Cottage. Where the track approaches the current railway, and just before arriving at a road, **turn L** through a hedge to visit The Navigation Inn.

To return, retrace your steps, but then continue on the main trail, ignoring two left turns back to the Bath Yard and Conkers. The disused railway is then followed over two bridges and back into Donisthorpe Woodland Park. Cross the bridge over a stream and continue straight on through the park to reach the road and gates visited on the outward journey. Cross the road to the continuation of the trail and return to Measham.

CONKERS

Conkers was previously the 'Heart of the National Forest' Visitor Centre and is now a leisure centre with information point and free parking. (Gates are closed at 6 pm during the summer months and earlier in winter.) Access can be gained here to Sarah's Wood, which was opened in 1995 and named after Sarah Louise Goudie, a girl with cerebral palsy who was then aged 5. Her family are supporters of Scope, a charity which helped to purchase the site and establish the woodland. The paths around the woodland are built for accessibility and a special playground and picnic site are designed with special needs in mind. Conkers is itself a discovery centre with over 100 interactive exhibits. Outdoors there are 120 acres of woodland trails and lakes, an adventure playground, assault course, toddlers' play area; also there are specialist shops, forest products outlet, craft workshops, a train ride, picnic areas, and restaurants.

ASHBY WOULDS HERITAGE TRAIL

This local history and nature trail is for use by pedestrians, cyclists, horseriders and people in wheelchairs. It links sites of local and industrial history including Moira Furnace, the former Donisthorpe colliery (now Donisthorpe Woodland Park), and the Moira Junction Nature Reserve. The trail runs along the former Ashby and Nuneaton joint railway which opened in 1873 and was built to transport coal from local pits to London and the south east. The line closed to regular passenger traffic in 1931 and the last goods train ran in 1981.

MOIRA FURNACE

Moira Furnace is an early 19th-century blast furnace. It originally opened in 1806 to extract iron ore from the coal deposit

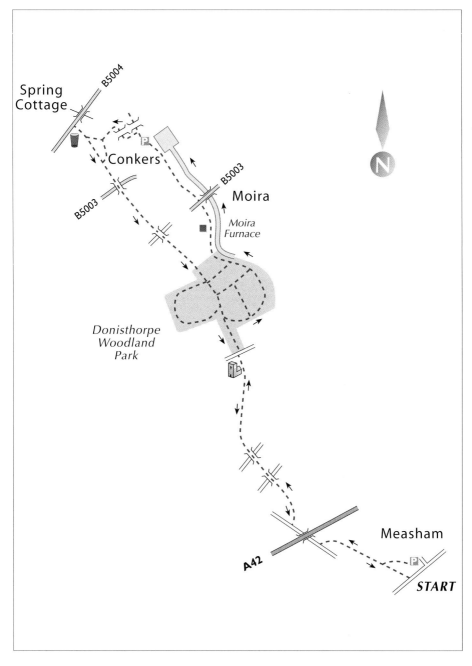

Moira furnace, now an interesting museum

A length of the recently restored Ashby Canal

already mined in the Ashby Woulds area. The furnace was only operational for 11 months due to variability in quantity and quality but was restarted in 1810, for a period of just nine months. Moira Furnace site was restored in 2000 and is now open to the public as a museum alongside restored limekilns and craft workshops.

DONISTHORPE WOODLAND PARK
This wood was created on the site of Donisthorpe colliery, one of the last deep mines to close. It is an area of approximately 75 acres with a variety of footpaths and cycle routes and has been planted with around 74,000 trees.

MEASHAM
Measham is a small industrial town developed around mining in the 19th and 20th centuries. It was one of the birthplaces of the industrial revolution due largely to the efforts of Joseph

Wilkes, who bought the manor around 1777. He was a captain of industry and commerce, a banker, coal mine owner brick producer and mill owner. In Measham he introduced the first steam engine in the area, a Boulton and Watts engine for his corn mill. He virtually rebuilt Measham, and the modern look of the village can be largely accredited to him.

THE ASHBY DE LA ZOUCH CANAL
The canal was completed in 1804 and ran without locks for 30 miles from Bedworth in Warwickshire to just north of Moira. Subsidence caused the canal to be diverted in 1918. In 1944 it was abandoned from its northern terminus to Donisthorpe due to further subsidence. There is now a project in place to reclaim the canal and it is being restored in stages from Snarestone to Moira. A boat trip operates at certain times.

Market Bosworth and the Battlefield

18½ miles

Market Bosworth is inextricably linked with that most famous of English battles, the Battle of Bosworth Field, where Richard of York finally did give battle in vain. A memorial in Richard's Field, passed early on the ride, marks the spot where Richard III died – a scene immortalised by Shakespeare's line 'a horse, a horse, my kingdom for a horse'. The award winning Battlefield Visitor Centre tells the full story and brings those distant events back to life. Away from the battlefield there are plenty of other attractions, including a heritage railway, several crossings of the Ashby Canal (three over and one under) and the pretty town of Market Bosworth.

Map: OS Landranger 140

Starting point: Bosworth Battlefield Visitor Centre. At the time of writing car parking costs £1. GR 403002

By train: Hinckley, from where the route can be joined at Wykin in approximately 2 miles.

Refreshments: There is a Buttery at the Visitor Centre serving snacks and meals, and Market Bosworth is a small town with all facilities. There are also pubs in several of the villages *en route*.

The route: A moderately easy ride in gentle hills. The ride sticks to minor roads but traffic can be busy near the Battlefield Visitor Centre and Market Bosworth.

From the car park return down the hill to the road and **turn L**, signed for Shenton Station. Pass under the railway bridge and **turn L**, signed for Dadlington and Stoke Golding, heading towards the station. Immediately on the right is Richard's Field and memorial stone. At the top of a short climb Shenton station is on the left. Continue, crossing the Asby de la Zouch canal, to a 'Give Way' at a crossroads, where go straight ahead heading for Dadlington.

Re-cross the canal and keep with the main road through Dadlington, passing the church and sign for the Dog and Hedgehog. At a crossroads continue straight ahead into Stoke Golding, and at a T-junction **turn R**, heading for Higham on the Hill and Fenny Drayton. At the next T-junction **turn L** onto Wykin Lane heading for Wykin.

Shenton station on the Battlefield line – a possible refreshment stop on the ride

On reaching Wykin, on the outskirts of Hinckley, **turn R** onto Higham Lane, pass a fishery on the right and at the next junction, just before the canal bridge, **turn R** onto Basin Bridge Lane, signed for Upton. Continue alongside the canal for a little way before **turning L** with the road, crossing the canal via Basin Bridge and immediately crossing a second bridge, over a dismantled railway.

Continue to a 'Give Way' at a crossroads and go straight ahead, still heading for Upton. Cross a further bridge over the dismantled railway and **turn L** at the next junction, signed for Fenny Drayton and Upton. **Turn L** again at the next junction, still heading for Fenny Drayton and Upton, and

almost immediately **turn R** for Upton.

Continue into Upton, pass the Upton Barn country restaurant and pub, and just beyond the phone box where the road bends to the left **turn R**, heading for Shenton. **Turn R** in Shenton and then **turn L** over the marsh signed for Sutton Cheney and the Battlefield Visitor Centre, passing the church on the left and going under the aqueduct carrying the canal.

At the T-junction by the aqueduct a **R turn** offers a short cut back to the Visitor Centre, or **turn L**, signed for Far Coton to continue the route. **Turn L** again at the next junction, also signed for Far Coton, and at a junction by a canal bridge

89

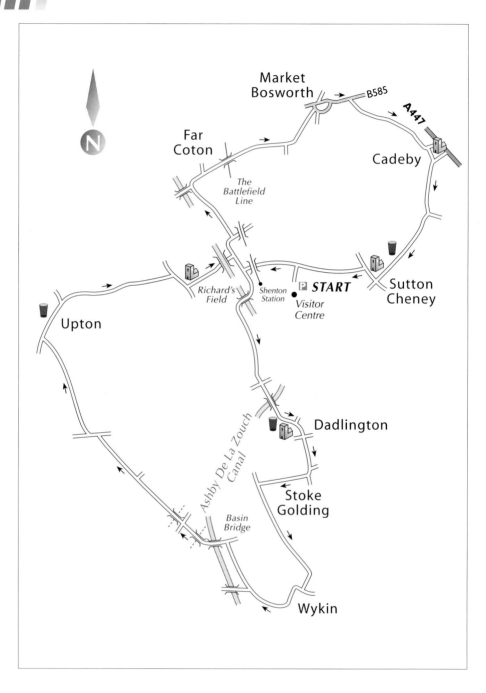

turn R, signed for Far Coton and Market Bosworth.

Continue into Far Coton and at the junction keep right heading for Market Bosworth. Cross over the Battlefield Line and at a 'Give Way' **turn L** and into Market Bosworth.

At the next 'Give Way' in the town **turn L**, heading for the town centre, then **turn R** onto Main Street, signed for Cadeby and almost immediately **turn R** again onto Park Street by Ye Olde Red Lion. Keep left with the road by the park, passing Bosworth Hall Hotel on the left and Bosworth Country Park on the right, and then **turn R** onto Cadeby Road, heading for Cadeby, passing a tearoom on the left.

In Cadeby, before the road meets the A447, **turn R** onto the minor Church Lane. Pass the church on the left and at the next junction **turn R** onto Sutton Lane, signed for Sutton Cheney and Shenton. Continue to a 'Give Way', where **turn R** for Sutton Cheney and the Battlefield Centre.

In Sutton Cheney pass the Royal Arms Hotel and the Hercules pub and then **turn R**, to return to the Battlefield Centre and car park.

BOSWORTH BATTLEFIELD VISITOR CENTRE

The Visitor Centre is open every day from 1 April to 31 October from 11 am till 5 pm, also Sundays in November and December, and Saturdays and Sundays in March. However, it may be closed if there is a special event taking place such as the English Civil War Battle re-enactment. The country park with its waymarked paths is open all year.

THE BATTLEFIELD LINE

This railway has its southern terminus at Shenton Station, from where it runs the 5 miles to Shackerstone mostly alongside the Ashby canal. The Shackerstone Railway Society maintains the tracks, vehicles and gardens and also provides engine drivers, guards and signalmen. Trains run from March to the end of October most weekends, and can also be booked for an extra special birthday party or wedding!

SHENTON STATION

Shenton Station provides a battlefield information point; also a local potter; café and toilets can be found here.

RICHARD'S FIELD

Richard's Field can be found to the west at the bottom of the hill before Shenton Station and is where Richard 3rd was killed in the Battle of Bosworth Field. The plaque reads, 'Richard, the last Plantagenet King of England, was slain here 22nd August 1485.'

20

Sence Valley Forest Park, Ibstock

3 miles

Cycling amenities resulting from the redevelopment of disused industrial facilities have featured heavily in this guide, and this route offers another good example. This part of the Sence Valley was once home to a 180-acre open-cast coal mine, but now plays host to an increasing variety and quantity of bird life. The tracks around the park's lakes and through its young woodland, which forms part of the National Forest, offer pleasant cycling for young and old alike.

Map: OS Explorer 245

Starting point: The main parking area in the Forest Park. Note there is a height restriction on the park entrance, so take bikes off car roofs before entering. There are toilets and an information board by the start. The information board includes a map of permitted cycle routes and also the route of a bridleway passing through the park (also available to cyclists). If exploring please stick to these routes. GR 403114

By train: No convenient station.

Refreshments: There is a pub in Heather.

The route: A very short, partly off-road, introductory ride. The tracks available for cycling within the forest park are limited, but offer a safe environment for novice cyclists to gain confidence before venturing further afield. As ever, be considerate of other trail users – this is a popular pedestrian and dog walking venue. Also take care as vehicles use the track between the upper and lower car parks. The road section used outside the park can be busy, especially the hill back down into the valley from Heather.

Return towards the exit and **turn L** onto the road that descends to the car park for the disabled and day fishers. Begin to descend and shortly, on a left-hand bend, **turn R** on a bridleway leading to the park edge. Take care here as vehicles using the lower car park may be encountered.

At the edge of the forest park **turn L** onto a rough track which is a public byway. This leads through an area of disused workings, now grazed farmland, and over the River Sence to a junction with a minor road, where **turn L** with care.

On the cycle track in Sence Valley Forest Park

Follow the road into Heather, where **turn L** at the mini-roundabout, heading for Ibstock. Take extra care on this busier stretch of road. Note – there is a footpath on the right for small children if required. Descend and just after crossing the bridge in the valley bottom dismount and **turn L**, walking with your bike on the public footpath signed for Ravenstone. The footpath leads immediately to a junction with the old road, where **turn R** and through the bridle gate back into the Sence Valley Forest Park.

Continue straight ahead and through the gate at the next junction, crossing the bridge between Goss Water and Horseshoe Lake. **Keep R** at the next junction, over the river, and then **R again**, keeping with the cycleable track. By the lower car park pass through the gate and **turn L** to climb back to the upper car park.

• •

SENCE VALLEY FOREST PARK

This 150-acre woodland and wildlife haven has been created from a disused opencast working. It includes broad-leaved and conifer woodland, several large lakes and conservation grassland. One hundred and fifty species of bird have been recorded since 1995 and can be observed from a hide overlooking the lakeland area. The park has trails for walkers, cyclists, horse-riders and disabled visitors, with free car parking.

93

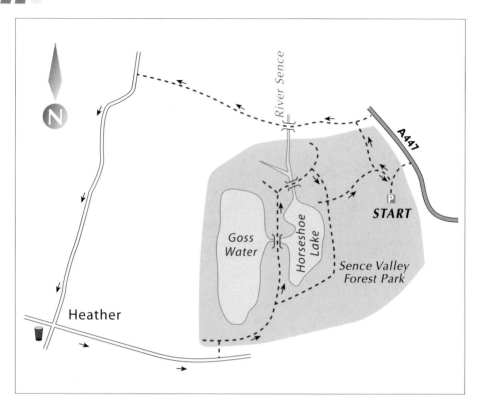

BIRDLIFE

Leicester and Rutland Ornithological Society have an extremely successful habitat at Sence Valley Forest Park, which comes into its own in winter. Double figures of stonechats have been recorded as well as winter finch and bunting flocks containing some corn buntings. The continued growth of the newly planted trees has encouraged small flocks of lesser redpolls. Short-eared owl, merlin, buzzard and the occasional peregrine have also been seen. Although this is not really a wildfowl site, some gosander and wigeon have visited. In spring and autumn the site is the best in the country for wheatears and whinchats, and redstarts are regularly found.

An owl keeps watch in the Park

FURTHER INFORMATION

As you get more involved, you will probably want to keep up to date with what is happening locally and nationally on the cycling scene. The popular press is dominated by mountain bike magazines, but more all-round titles, notably *Cycling Plus*, do exist and are a good starting point for national information. Most good newsagents will stock a suitable title.

The National Cycling Network has been big news in recent years, and Sustrans – the sustainable transport charity driving this – are active locally as well as nationally. Their web site and newsletters provide an overview and updates on the network, and maps and books cover the detail. The major routes passing through Leicester and Rutland areas are routes 6, 63 and 64.

There are many other cycle rides described for this area and local Tourist Information Centres will have details, maps and guides.

Nationally, the Cycle Touring Club (CTC) is the largest cycling organisation and local groups in the area organise rides and social events.

Contact details:
Sustrans: PO Box 21, Bristol, BS99 2HA.
www.sustrans.org.uk

CTC: Cotterell House, 69 Meadrow, Godalming, Surrey. GU7 3HS.
www.ctc.org.uk